SOUL
ECHOES

SOUL ECHOES

THE HEALING POWER
OF PAST-LIFE THERAPY

THELMA B. FREEDMAN, Ph.D.

CITADEL PRESS
Kensington Publishing Corp.
www.kensingtonbooks.com

CITADEL PRESS BOOKS are published by

Kensington Publishing Corp.
850 Third Avenue
New York, NY 10022

All Kensington titles, imprints, and distributed lines are available at special quantity discounts for bulk purchases for sales promotions, premiums, fund-raising, educational, or institutional use. Special book excerpts or customized printings can also be created to fit specific needs. For details, write or phone the office of the Kensington special sales manager: Kensington Publishing Corp., 850 Third Avenue, New York, NY 10022, attn: Special Sales Department, phone 1-800-221-2647.

First printing: January 2002

10 9 8 7 6 5 4 3 2 1

Printed in the United States of America

Library of Congress Control Number: 2001094197

ISBN 0-8065-2209-7

This book is dedicated to my family, who have given me encouragement to continue as a past life therapist, to my mentors Drs. Stanley Krippner, Thomas Greening, and Donald Rothberg, and to the many past-life therapists who have become my friends and colleagues over the years. Thank you all.

CONTENTS

FOREWORD

Thelma Freedman has honored me by asking me to write this foreword to her book. I have known her for a number of years, as a colleague; a member of APRT, the Association for Past-Life Research and Therapies—including a stint together on the APRT Board of Directors; as my coeditor of the *Journal of Regression Therapy;* and most assuredly, as a friend. It is my considered belief that no one I know has a greater knowledge of the research and writing being done in the field of past-life therapy than Thelma. Thus, I feel she is well qualified to write a book such as this and has done so lovingly and passionately, sharing ideas, concepts, theories, and case studies with the reader.

This book is a collection of Thelma's experiences as a past-life therapist, filled with gems of common sense and caveats for clients and practitioners alike. It is richly illustrated with explanations and excerpts from the case studies of work she has done over the years with some of her clients. In content, it is suitable for both the interested casual reader and the demanding professional, a rare combination indeed.

To read this book is to hear Thelma's voice. She writes very much as she speaks: low-keyed yet passionate, straight-to-the-point and pragmatic. No pussyfooting here. Thelma tells it like it is from the perspective of an experienced past-life therapist who has been in the trenches, not off somewhere thinking up dandy theories and grand ideas with no practical experience to back them up.

Because of her plain talk and knowledge, her words will be of special importance to anyone interested in the interrelated topics of psychology, reincarnation, and past-life therapy. She understands that these topics are tied one to the other in the real world and cannot exist as neat little individual, independent subjects. It is only in the acceptance of this interrelationship that all three can be better understood, especially when they are subjected to Thelma's insightful examination and clear explanation.

It is not to say that every person who reads this book will agree with all that is written herein. Obviously, there are some who will, doubtless, take umbrage with her perspective here and there. So be it. Thelma herself speaks to the issue of perspective and what are "reality" and "truth." They, just like concepts such as religion and the roles of a government, are tightly bound to the group or society in which these concepts are being viewed. For an individual or a society, perspective equals truth. In my own practice, I have noted that the roots of dissension are often based on perspective, and I would like to use a simple illustration from my own youth. In the little Midwestern town in which I grew up, there was a man who was a bit different. (May I digress to point out that if one has money and is strange, then he or she is labeled "eccentric" but, if poor, is simply labeled "crazy.") So, this crazy guy painted his car in such a manner that, if viewed from the driver's side, it appeared to be bright yellow, but if viewed from the passenger side, it looked wine red. Thus the problem of perspective. The color of the car was determined by where you stood, and while "truth" appeared to be supported by your perspective, all was not as it appeared to be and great arguments resulted. So, too, with many of the concepts Thelma explores. It is her goal to recognize the frailties of limited perspectives and to replace them with the "truth" as she knows it.

So, one might ask, why should I read this book? First, because Thelma has something to say and she writes from a standpoint of experience in and knowledge of her subject. It is based on many years of diligent studies, research, and practice, not least of which was the completion of a doctorate in clinical psychology and years of editorship on the *Journal of Regression Therapy*. Second, she has an ability to explain complex concepts in a clear and understandable fashion. Unlike many books on the subject, this one is written in a clear and lucid style that makes complex issues easier to understand. Third, what she says is practical and makes sense, often an all-too-rare quality in much of what is foisted off on readers today. Fourth, it is an enjoyable as well as an informative read. To read it is to come away better informed and to want to keep this book handy to reread and occasionally to thumb through it with the question, "Let me think now, what did Thelma say about that?"

Russell C. Davis, Ph.D.

Dr. Russell Davis practiced past-life therapy for many years, and served as an editor of the Journal of Regression Therapy *as well as on the Board of Directors of the Association for Past Life Research and Therapies (now the International Association for Research and Regression Therapies (IARRT). He kindly wrote this foreword shortly before his passing, and in tribute to his memory and his friendship I include it.*

INTRODUCTION

I have been a past-life therapist for over twenty years; I work with people in individual sessions as well as in group workshops. Soon after I became a hypnotherapist, I became intrigued when a hypnotized client slipped back into a past-life spontaneously. At that time I knew nothing about past lives except that people did sometimes report them in hypnosis. So when my client began talking about sitting on a hillside (she thought it was in Spain) wearing a long old-fashioned dress, I realized that this was one of those strange things, a past-life regression, but I didn't know what I should do about it. I brought her back to the present and woke her, and we set her second appointment for two weeks later.

I spent that time trying to educate myself about past-life regression. It seems hard to believe today, but that was the middle 1970s and there was precious little available then. I could find only one book. But it was partly about past-life therapy and it told me what I needed to know. Two weeks later, when my client came in for that next session, we proceeded, and in hypnosis she went back to that hillside in Spain. We moved on from there, discovering the whole sad past-life story.

That was interesting, but I was not sure the experience had helped her in any way until a few weeks had passed and she told me that she no longer had the lifelong problem she had come to see me about in the first place! When I learned of the almost miraculous cure her past-life regression had wrought, I was impressed, and I have become more and more impressed in the years since then. I discuss her case in more detail in Chapter 10.

Since then, I have used past-life therapy with just about every kind of problem conceivable. It is not always relevant: sometimes problems are caused by physical conditions or experiences in this present life. But when it is relevant, its results are almost magical. By the end of the 1970s, other books had begun to appear about past-life regression. I devoured them all. Some research was carried out, too, by Dr. Helen Wambach, and I studied her work carefully. I also discovered the work of Dr. Ian Stevenson, who investigated cases of young children who seemed to remember their past lives without the help of hypnosis. Then in 1980, the Association for Past-Life Research and Therapies was formed. I joined immediately, of course, and found wonderful friends who were as "crackpot" as I.

I say "crackpot" because back in those days that's what a dabbler in past-life therapy was considered to be by the psychological community at large. In fact, it is fair to say that we are still considered "crackpots" by many in that community, although some go further and use the word "charlatan." Some, but not all. More and more psychologists, psychiatrists, and other counselors are using past-life therapy these days; they may not believe that these stories are "real" past lives, but they have found that they help their clients at least as much as and sometimes more than other, more conventional, forms of therapy. Some use past-life therapy openly and say so, more use it secretly and whisper it only to sympathetic ears, but whether in the closet or out, more and more mental health professionals are using it every year.

Over the years, I have naturally wondered which of our theories in psychology made sense from the standpoint of the past-life stories people told and the fact that these stories were therapeutic. I also wondered about that therapeutic quality itself: Why are they therapeutic? These questions can be asked if past-life stories are memories of real past lives or if they are fantasies.

For years, I myself "sat on the fence" about the reality or fantasy issue, and refused to take a stand, because the question had been neither tested nor proven either way. But recent research, my own and others', as well as the sheer weight of the evidence now coming from hundreds of therapists all over the world, has made me realize that past-life stories are more likely real than not, more likely to be memories than fantasies.

In this book I take the position that they are real, knowing that I may be wrong. But oddly enough, they fit better with some current psychological theories if they are real than if they are fantasies.

This is not to say that *all* past-life stories are real. Some are clearly fantasies, often delightful fantasies, but fantasies nonetheless. And even those that are real may well be mixed with some elements of fantasy; that's the way human memory is, even for memories of events in our present lives. Like many people, you may have had the experience of going back to some familiar place after many years and being surprised at how inaccurately you had remembered it. Still, you *had* remembered it, in its basic outlines, even if you got some of the details wrong. Past-life stories may be like that: real memories, but remembered a bit askew, with some of the details missing or wrong and some perhaps added. But the general outline is there, and perhaps the person was really there, long ago.

In this book you will read of many past lives, all over the world and time. Several chapters deal with therapy for various conditions, and in each one you will find descriptions of past lives that were connected with those conditions. The first three chapters present brief overviews of reincarnation belief systems, psychological theories that seem relevant, and past-life regression and therapy, and in the last chapter I try to pull it all together. I may or may not be successful in this; you must judge. But past-life regression itself is a field in which every answer leads to another question, and sometimes more than one question, and we are just beginning to understand what they show us about ourselves.

This book is about past-life regression stories, reincarnation, and psychology. It is an attempt to tie those areas together into some framework that makes sense. We live in a time when a good many people in our scientific Western world have become dissatisfied with the old tried-and-true ways of looking at life, at other people, and at themselves. What is called the "New Age" is flourishing, as more people every day feel themselves to be spiritually impoverished and begin to look for answers not provided by our more conventional, respectable ways of thinking.

In this book you will find many past lives examined, from many people, to show how we seem to grow, how we get sick, and how we heal. None of these past lives are of famous or particularly important people; no Cleopatras here, no kings or queens, no architects of pyramids. Simple folk, for the most part, living their lives as well as they could and dying bitterly or happily, with lessons learned or not learned, with goals accomplished or not, and whether they were ready or not.

This is not a zany book about zany stuff. Here you will find no guardian angels leading people into higher realms of existence; no possessing spirits or not-so-friendly ghosts; no Akashic records of all one's lives, past, present, or future; no speculations about parallel universes; no beings of light; no extraterrestrial aliens sent to save us from ourselves. This book is based upon what people actually report in past-life regressions, not my theories or anyone else's. I have drawn on the past-life stories my clients have related, with their permission, of course, and I have given them fictitious names.

Nor is this a book on religious beliefs about reincarnation. There are hundreds of different theories about how reincarnation is believed to occur, and most of them contradict others. You will find none of them in this book, except for the first chapter, which is a fast overview of the various major reincarnationist belief systems.

I have tried to keep this book sensible. It reflects what we actually know, from two areas of research and the experience of numerous therapists. The two areas are the past-life memories that emerge under hypnosis, and the memories of prior lives related by young children without hypnosis. There is both empirical and anecdotal evidence in both of these areas, and I have tried to wed that evidence with what we know about human life.

Thus, if wild and wooly speculation is what you want, this book is not for you.

To some, it may look like wild and wooly speculation even to suggest that reincarnation could, in fact, occur at all. Yet the evidence indicates that it may very well occur, and that our experiences in our past lives shape us now, in our present lives, to a great degree. Obviously, this concept would have a powerful influence on psychology and would interact with it. When it is relevant, you will find that influence and that interaction examined in this book.

This is not a religious book. Indeed, some might call it an irreligious book, because of its perhaps grubby insistence upon life as we know it, here and now and in the past on this very earth. Reincarnation, as it actually appears to happen based upon the two types of apparent memories mentioned seems earth-based, and fits into several already-existing paradigms of science.

And now I contradict myself and admit that I do indulge in some speculation in the final chapters. It is my belief, based upon the evidence of recent Gallup polls, that reincarnation will soon become the prevailing belief system throughout the Western world, as it already is throughout the East. If this is correct, it is truly time to speculate: we should begin to speculate upon what kind of society we can and will create, based upon that belief.

Many societies have been based upon or incorporated reincarnation belief systems, and a good many of them were rather dreadful places in which we, today, would not choose to live. In other words, belief in reincarnation does not in itself make a society a good one. In fact, it could conceivably make it cruel and uncaring. But it does not have to end that way, and because this can be avoided, we should try to find the good that can come from reincarnation belief and to work toward a good society based upon it.

There are a good many questions raised in this book that no one can answer because no one knows the answers yet. I throw these questions out to you, the reader, as challenges to your curiosity and to your willingness to participate in the ancient enterprise of trying to create the good society we all want.

SOUL
ECHOES

CHAPTER ONE

A BRIEF OVERVIEW OF REINCARNATION

Reincarnation is one of the oldest beliefs in the world. It reaches back into prehistory, and has been part of the religious beliefs of people all over the globe. In fact, *disbelief* in reincarnation is recent in the long millennia of human existence. Only in the Western world where official Christianity has spread has reincarnation been considered impossible, ridiculous, or heretical. In fact, to the official Roman Catholic Church, belief in it is still technically considered a heresy.

There have been many names for reincarnation, coming from many times and places. These terms include: metempsychosis, palingenesis, preexistence, transmigration, rebirth, punar-janman, again birth, samsara, and the wheel of births and deaths. Many animal symbols have represented reincarnation, too: birds, butterflies, serpents, salamanders, and dragons, to name a few. Various plants and stones, for instance the lotus and the moonstone, have also symbolized reincarnation, as have symbols of the sun, the moon, and the seasonal cycles of the earth and the planets. All of these symbols appear in many forms in native arts and often originally symbolized a belief in reincarnation.

But perhaps the most powerful symbol everywhere, and the one that appears most frequently, is the wheel, symbolizing, of course, the endless cycle of birth, death, and rebirth. Circles and mandalas, both stylized wheels, are found in many cultures' art and mythology, and usually refer to an ancient belief in reincarnation, even if the present people no longer hold that belief.

The circle is sometimes augmented with some other powerful symbol, in two cases at least, the cross. This is the case with the Egyptian ankh, originally a symbol for life, the afterlife, and eternal rebirth. Although the ankh contains both a circle and a cross, the cross of the ankh predates the Christian cross by centuries.

A later circle and cross combination, still used today, is the Coptic Cross, the cross with the circle surrounding the crux. The early Coptic Christians were Gnostic Christians, a reincarnationist group of Christians who combined Greek and Eastern teachings with Christ's in the first few centuries after Christ's death. The familiar circle on the Coptic Cross is a symbol for reincarnation within Christianity. In the sixth century, when the Roman Catholic Church declared belief in reincarnation anathema, the circle on the cross was forbidden. But the Eastern Catholic Churches still use it, and some small groups within them are still reincarnationists.

Belief in some form of reincarnation was part of many primitive religions, although not everyone was always thought to reincarnate. In many systems, only the leaders, special heroes, or shamans or priests reincarnated. And of course, in many systems, women were not included. There were also differences in the number of times people were thought to reincarnate, ranging from only three times to thousands.

Anthropologists studying indigenous peoples today find that reincarnation beliefs are still common, although details differ. On all continents, many indigenous peoples have assumed that reincarnation occurs in one form or another. This is true of many Native American people as well as traditional people from South and Central America, Africa, Australia, the Pacific Islands, and the Arctic Circle. In some of these systems people are thought to reincarnate as animals, in others, not. And in some, people are believed to reincarnate only into their own families, while in others they move from family to family. In some systems, also, people reincarnate immediately after death, but in others a certain time must pass, and sometimes certain rites must be performed before they can reincarnate. But underlying all these variations is the universal, ancient belief in reincarnation.

ANCIENT EUROPE

Reincarnation was a common belief in the part of the ancient world we now call Europe. Although we sometimes think of the Celts as people of the British Isles, they actually had spread over most of Northern Europe long before the Romans arrived. As a group, they were so successful for so long that by the time the Romans began their march northward into Europe, the Celts had subdivided into regional groups, which the Romans called by different names. For example, the "Gauls" (who lived in what we now call France) were originally a branch of the Celts.

Each Celtic branch had developed its own different customs and identities, but they were also alike in many ways and one way was their common belief in reincarnation. We know from Roman writings that in the British Isles, as in the rest of Europe, the belief was still strong when the Romans arrived. And Julius Caesar, in his *Gallic War, Book VI,* comments upon the Gauls' fearlessness in war, which he attributes to their belief in reincarnation.

The Celts' great common symbols were the circle and its variant, the spiral. Some consider the spiral more sophisticated than the circle because it implies continuous change and growth through repeated lives rather than the repetition that a circle suggests. When archeologists dig in the deep ancient graves of Europe, they find circles and spirals of gold and silver and iron, beautifully wrought, some intended to be worn as jewelry or closures for clothing, some used as other decoration or for religious purposes.

Although they were not Celts originally, the ancient people of Scandinavia and the Germanic people were believers in reincarnation, and this belief has come into our own time in their epic poems; Wagner's Ring of the Nibelung operas as well as the poems of some of the great German poets used these mythic stories as themes. In the Scandinavian and Germanic systems, people were believed to reincarnate into the same family a short time after death. They also used the spiral as well as the circle as a major symbol, possibly borrowed from the Celts around them.

EGYPT

The ancient Egyptians, of course, believed that their pharaohs reincarnated after a time in the afterlife; it was partly the need for ensuring the comfort of the pharaoh in the afterlife that made the elaborate pyramidal tombs necessary. But this afterlife was not to be permanent: at the proper time, the pharaoh would reincarnate as another great pharaoh. Part of the worship of Osiris involved the belief that at certain times, when they were badly needed, "great souls" would return to lead mankind out of whatever misery they had managed to get themselves into. The idea of great souls continually reincarnating in times of need is found in other systems, as we shall see.

As for ordinary mortals in ancient Egypt, after death their souls were weighed by the goddess Maat, who used a feather as a balance weight. If their sins were slight enough so that their souls were lighter than the feather, they could enter the kingdom of Osiris, where they got to serve the gods and the great souls waiting in the afterlife. If not, it was into everlasting darkness for them. But either way, ordinary people did not reincarnate.

ASIA

Meanwhile, on the Asian continent, reincarnation had been the common belief for centuries. As in Europe, it is impossible to know when this belief began in Asia because it existed long before written records began. It is still part of most Asian religions, and has been for thousands of years. Today the two largest, of course, are Hinduism and Buddhism. There are major differences between them.

Whereas Hinduism can be said to have created itself over centuries through numerous legends, poems, epic tales, and philosophical writings, Buddhism dates itself from the life and teachings of Gautama Buddha 2,500 years ago. By his own teaching, Gautama was but one of many Buddhas: the word "Buddha" is Sanskrit and means one who is "fully enlightened." There have been and will be many Buddhas.

Both Hinduism and Buddhism incorporated reincarnation into their belief systems, but with one important difference. Hindu reincarnation proceeds through a comparatively recent concept of "karma," which says that if you live a good life this time, you will reincarnate into a higher level of life next time. This idea has been perverted into the political concept of higher and lower social castes that shaped the Indian social system for centuries and still has influence today, fifty years after the caste system was made illegal. In addition, Hindu reincarnation belief holds that if you live a really evil life, your karma will be so bad that you will reincarnate into the body of an animal next time. And some groups within Hinduism hold that all souls must reincarnate as animals seven (or three, or ten) times before making it back to a human state. In Hinduism, the focus is on living a good life within the social class (or caste) you are born to in the hopes of rising to a better class next time. The good life requires respect for living things, doing your duty as defined by your class, and worshipping the gods and goddesses with the proper rites.

The focus of Buddhism is very different. It is more intellectual and also more spiritual and, these days, appeals more strongly to Western people. There are many schools of thought in Buddhism, and they differ in their attitudes about reincarnation. Contrary to popular belief, some early Buddhist schools actually *disbelieved* in personal reincarnation, particularly the early Theravada school.

This school interpreted the teachings of Buddha as meaning that there was no individual soul, merely ego, and that this ego stopped at death while the soul remained part of the greater soul, which produced another life. This new life, however, had no direct connection with the prior one. To give a simplistic analogy, if you scooped a glass of water from the sea, poured it back in, and waited a bit, then scooped out another glassful, it is unlikely that you would have in the glass any of the water molecules from the first glassful. In this sense, for Theravadan Buddhism, there is no continuation of one soul from life to life.

Mahayana Buddhism, however, which developed later and seems to have absorbed some of the teachings of Hinduism, considers the soul as independently existing prior to the body, actually creating the most appropriate body for its next incarnation. For them, the goal of reincarnation is to learn to let go of the ego and all its desires through many incarnations.

Mahayana Buddhists (and almost all Buddhists today) also believe that some souls reach perfection, or nearly so, but choose to be reborn to help others reach that goal. When one attains perfection, one can enter Nirvana, a state of ego-free blending with the universe. However, Gautama Buddha is said to have reached Nirvana and refused to cross into it, vowing to return to earth over and over until no soul remained unenlightened. There are three levels of beings who can make this choice: Arahats, Bodhisattvas, and Buddhas. For the first two, choosing to return to help others helps them also by moving them closer to Buddhahood; for a Buddha, the choice is an act of pure selflessness that nevertheless makes him or her even more deserving of Nirvana.

For all Buddhists, Gautama Buddha's message was that life is suffering, and the goal of life is the overcoming of desire and thus overcoming suffering. When this goal is finally reached, one enters Nirvana, unless one chooses to return to help others. Even for the Theravadan school, the attainment of perfection is the goal, and it takes many incarnations, as for them there is no direct connection from one incarnation to the next. Strictly speaking, traditionally Buddhists have considered reincarnation as a curse, a sign that perfection has not yet been reached so more suffering is in order.

Over the centuries, many offshoots of Buddhism have grown up, each with its own disciplines designed to help the seeker reach perfection. Although they differ, most teach methods to eliminate all desire from one's mind through meditation and all prescribe leading a simple, even an ascetic, life.

Zen Buddhism, a form of Mahayana Buddhism, is a bit different, and it has become popular in the West. Originating in China, spreading to Japan and now found throughout Asia, Zen Buddhism holds that enlightenment can be found in correctly living daily life as well as in meditation and withdrawal from the busy world. Especially important are the arts, and Zen Buddhism has had a profound influence upon Chinese and Japanese arts. For some Zen schools, creative art is considered the highest form one's daily life can take and thus the most enlightening form of meditation. Others, however, consider that all activities of daily life, even

the simplest footstep or a breath, offer opportunities for enlightenment and should be performed with reverence, attention, and
care.

Buddhism has branches in all Asian countries, and they have all
developed their own individual approaches. Today all Buddhists
can be said to take reincarnation for granted, and for most, it is a
personal reincarnation. Scholars argue over exactly what it is that
reincarnates: the character? the personality? the memory? But despite these philosophical differences, some form of personal reincarnation is the general belief.

Ancient Greece

Some of the ancient Greeks were strong believers in reincarnation, and many early writings deal with the possible mechanics of it.
It is likely that some of the Greek beliefs were "borrowed" from the
Egyptians and from the Asian continent; they had extensive contact with both. Plato was a strong believer in reincarnation, as was
Socrates, whom we know only through Plato's writings. It was
Socrates who said that "all knowledge is merely recollection of
things known before." Aristotle, on the other hand, although he
believed in reincarnation in his early writings, turned away from it
later and became an influential opponent.

Before any of them, Pythagoras was the founder of a reincarnationist school of philosophy; there is some confusion as to whether
or not he believed in reincarnation into animal bodies or not.
Scholars of our own time dispute this, and it is not a new argument
because scholars of Pythagoras' time disputed it, too. This may be
one of the longest-running arguments in the world: it's been going
on for 2,500 years!

Aside from the philosophers, the so-called Greek mystery
schools taught reincarnation. As everywhere else in Europe, belief
in reincarnation was common in Greece for at least 1,500 years
B.C.E. It flourished on all the islands long before there was a unified
Greece and continued to be a belief among "ordinary" people
until the fifth century C.E. when the last Eleusinian Mystery School
was suppressed. However, Aristotle's views opposing reincarnation

also spread throughout Greece, and by the first century B.C.E. most educated people, who had studied his ideas, rejected the concept, considering it fit only for common people, women, and slaves; and sure enough, many of them were faithful to it.

ROME

The attitudes of the educated Greeks were copied by educated Romans, as they copied so much else of Greek culture. But as was also true in Greece, the ordinary people believed in reincarnation, and it was not actively suppressed. As time passed, educated Romans also began to take it seriously. Cicero, especially, in the first century B.C.E., having noticed the prevalence of reincarnation belief everywhere the Romans went, "rediscovered" Pythagoras and Socrates and began to espouse the idea of reincarnation as a "respectable" one. Other Roman writers picked up the theme and made reincarnation a viable belief for educated Romans, or at least a respectable topic for philosophical discussion.

Belief in reincarnation, always existing among the common people, was augmented by the stream of people from other cultures that made Rome such a great city. In fact, in pre-Christian Rome one could have found just about every religious belief in the known world practiced by one group or another, and belief in reincarnation was part of many of them. Except for the practice of human sacrifice, which the Romans forbade and punished in all their territories, the Rome of those early days was tolerant of all religions as long as they were not revolutionary, so a belief in reincarnation was safe to hold. As the educated classes became interested, it also became respectable.

JUDAISM

One religion with which Rome came into contact was Judaism, often believed today to have no interest in reincarnation. However, this belief is incorrect. As is clear from the Old Testament, the ancient prophets were thought to be reincarnations of other, earlier, prophets. The Samaritans, especially, believed in reincarnation and traced the incarnations of Adam through Seth, Noah, and Abraham, to Moses. Some of the Dead Sea Scrolls, now slowly being translated, hint at reincarnation beliefs on the part of the Essenes. And today's scholars of mystical Judaism find in the ancient Kabbalah clear discussions of reincarnation. These scholars consider reincarnation and the Kabbalah as much a part of the teachings of Judaism as the Torah. Many suggestions of reincarnation can be found in early Judaic writings, but except for the Kabbalah, they point to an almost casual assumption rather than a well-developed system.

Over the millennia that Judaism has existed, reincarnation has risen and fallen in popular acceptance, but except for the Kabbalists, it has never had official sanction. The major exception is Hasidism, a movement that started in the eighteenth century in the Jewish ghettoes of Poland and that grew from old mystical traditions, including the study of the Kabbalah. Hasidism has spread to many countries, including the United States, where some adherents consider reincarnation as one of the central tenets of their faith. As for the better-known modern branches of Judaism, however, reincarnation is not officially accepted today. A good many modern Judaic scholars, however, are reexamining it.

ISLAM

Islam began in the seventh century C.E., when Mohammed presented to the world the Koran, which he said was revealed to him by Allah. The Koran contains many clear references to rebirth and the everlasting cycles of life, although Islamic scholars today place other meanings on these passages, interpreting them as riddles or parables. In the seventh century, at the time of Mohammed, the Middle East was a haven for people fleeing Europe and the persecutions of the Roman Christian Church, and many of these refugees were reincarnationists. They found many friendly minds awaiting them, for the Middle East was already strongly reincarnationist. As Islam spread during the next few centuries, it incorporated reincarnationist beliefs rather easily.

However, over time Islam has split into many branches, some remaining reincarnationist and others rejecting the concept. The two main branches are the Sunnis and the Shi'ites, both alive and well today. The Shi'ites have remained reincarnationist. Both of these branches have subdivided into many sects, however, and even within the Sunnis some sects are still reincarnationist.

Today, the largest single reincarnationist group within Islam are the Shi'ites; other groups are the Ismailis, the Sufis, and the Druse, a Lebanese branch of the Sufis. All have developed their own forms of reincarnation. There are three main kinds of reincarnation belief among Islamic groups: (1) the periodic incarnation of the perfect man or deity; (2) the continuous return of the Imam (spiritual leader) after death; and (3) the reincarnation of the souls of ordinary men. None of these categories includes women.

The Ismailis believe that the Hindu God Krishna (himself said to be an incarnation, or avatar, of another Hindu God, Vishnu) reincarnated as Gautama Buddha and then as Mohammed, and will return again. Other groups believe that the world is never without one of the Great Souls, always here to guide and direct human life. And two groups, at least, believe that Christ, after founding Christianity, again reincarnated as the founders of their particular sects.

Reincarnation is still alive in Islam, although orthodox scholars tend to ignore it. And indeed, the majority of Muslims today probably ignore it too. But it is certainly not suppressed or even discouraged. Those who continue to believe in it are fully accepted, and some reincarnation groups, for example the Sufis, are held in high regard by all Muslims. The Sufis are spiritual and scholarly in their approach; they hold that there is essentially only one universal truth, and that this truth can be apprehended by means of any and all religious creeds. This belief, plus their belief in the perfectibility of all mankind, may be part of the reason that Sufi groups have grown rapidly in Europe and the United States in recent years.

CHRISTIANITY

When discussing Judaism, I mentioned that the Jewish prophets were often thought to be reincarnations of earlier prophets or teachers. One "prophet" who was thought by his own disciples to be a possible incarnation of one of the ancient prophets was Jesus Christ. His disciples asked him whether he was Elias returned; in answer, Jesus said that Elias had returned but as John the Baptist, not himself. This is only one of many statements by Jesus or his disciples that indicate a belief in reincarnation. Many early Christians believed that Christ's message was reincarnation, not resurrection as usually understood today. Since reincarnation was a commonly accepted part of so many other religions of the time, it is not surprising that it was so easily accepted as part of Christ's teaching.

Reincarnation grew in popularity among Christians as part of their belief for the first two centuries after Christ's death. The belief may have grown in part because it was there to begin with, but also because the expected apocalypse and general resurrection, which the very early Christians expected to occur momentarily, did not occur at all. As time went by, it became reasonable to assume that reincarnation had been Christ's true message. In the third century the belief was adopted by the Bishop Origen, a Greek theologian, Platonist, and Gnostic Christian. His views were rapidly accepted by some of the other early church fathers during the next two centuries or so.

There were, however, many serious schisms in the early church over reincarnation and other issues, and in c.e. 543, the Emperor Justinian, desiring a consistent set of beliefs for a strong central church, convened a synod in Constantinople that, after some wrangling, condemned the teachings of Origen and some other scholars, including their teachings on reincarnation. Ten years later Justinian and the Fifth Ecumenical Council issued anathemas against Origen and all his teachings, including reincarnation. This second action effectively made belief in reincarnation a heresy, and it has not been rescinded yet.

These actions solidified an "acceptable" dogma for Christianity itself, as Justinian had hoped, creating an approved set of beliefs that could be taught by a strong central church as it spread around the world. Belief in reincarnation among Christians persisted underground, however, despite the heavy punishments, including death, that were meted out. Many Christian mystic groups throughout Europe and the Middle East kept their reincarnation beliefs as well as numerous beliefs from other ancient religions. As mentioned above, some of the refugees from the Church's persecutions fled to the Middle East during the sixth and seventh centuries and influenced the reincarnationist beliefs of the fledgling Islam. For over a thousand years dissident Christian groups rose and fell, always persecuted by the Church. Nevertheless, they sprang up again.

Perhaps the persecuted group best known to us today were the Cathars, a Christian reincarnationist sect that began in the twelfth century in Albigensia in Southern France and spread rapidly over southern and western Europe. During the thirteenth century, the Origensian, or Albigensian, heresy, as their belief was called, spread so fast that the Church mounted a campaign to "exterminate" all these heretics. This campaign was horrifically successful. Tens of thousands were imprisoned, tortured, and burned, and Catharism was finished. Some small, scattered reincarnationist groups sprang up over the next 300 years, but the Inquisition of the sixteenth century took care of them. After that, reincarnationist belief was effectively stamped out in Christian Europe for the next 300 years.

But reincarnation is stubborn, and it always lives up to its name. In the nineteenth century it was reborn in Europe, this time able to flourish better because the Church no longer had the political and military power to suppress it, although belief in it is technically still a heresy for Catholics and has no part in Protestantism either. Nevertheless, during the present century, belief in reincarnation has enjoyed a steady growth throughout the Western world. We people of the Western cultures are, of course, just catching up to the rest of the world, where reincarnation has never been doubted and rarely been persecuted.

There is an organized Christian movement in the modern Western world that espouses reincarnation, the Theosophist movement. Organized in 1875 to follow the mystical teachings of Helena

Blavatsky, the movement blends Western science with Eastern reincarnation and mystical beliefs. Basically, Theosophists see the reincarnating soul as going through a process of soul evolution, moving from life to life and learning as it goes. This part of their beliefs is actually reflected in what we see in past-life regression and therapy. Eventually, when the soul has learned all it must, Theosophists believe it will unite with God and have no more need to reincarnate. This idea blends the Hindu idea of a personal soul with the Buddhist idea of eventual perfection, but in Theosophism, perfection results in conscious unity with God instead of a state of ego-free (and thus consciousness-free) Nirvana, as in the Buddhist system.

This system seems to free reincarnation belief from the Hindu idea of karma, in which rewards and punishments flow automatically from one's actions. Since in the Hindu system bad actions (resulting in bad karma) are often unknown to the person doing them, for example stepping on an ant, there seems little hope for eventual redemption. The Theosophist system is based on learning lessons rather than a mindless reward and punishment system, and may seem fairer and more attractive to Western minds. Also, Western minds, ego-ridden as we are, may not much like the Buddhist idea of complete personal annihilation when the state of Nirvana is finally attained. In any case, Theosophism has grown slowly but steadily over the years in Europe and the United States, and its ideas have helped shape modern Western reincarnation beliefs.

TODAY IN THE WEST

According to a Gallup poll in June, 2001, 25 percent of Americans definitely believe in reincarnation and 20 percent are not sure. This means that 45 percent of Americans believe that reincarnation is at least a possibility. In Europe, the figures are higher. Although some Western reincarnationists today have become Buddhist, Sufi, or Theosophist, or have joined other, smaller, reincarnationist groups, many more are of the individual and independent variety, who read, seek, and take classes on their own, deciding for themselves what they believe and what they don't. This is wonderfully American and may actually give reincarnation the strength to withstand all the assaults that are still levied upon it from the orthodoxies of science as well as of religion.

The danger to reincarnation belief today is still probably greater from the religious side than the scientific side, as it always has been. For one thing, many scientists are actually beginning to entertain the idea of reincarnation. This is especially true of many mental health professionals, who are finding past-life therapy immensely useful, as you will see in later chapters. But it is also true of some cutting-edge physicists, who find bemusing things happening with the subatomic particles they themselves investigate. And in general, although some in the scientific community will certainly continue to scoff at the idea of reincarnation, like most scientists, they do support the general principle of freedom of belief. The dangerous attacks come and will come in the immediate future from the fundamentalist Christian sects, still as determined as the Roman Catholic Church ever was to stamp out belief in reincarnation, and perhaps not so scrupulous as scientists about stamping out freedom of religion as well.

One thing is for certain. Even if reincarnation belief is suppressed in the West during, say, the next century, it will eventually rise again, as it always has. Rebirth, after all, is what reincarnation is all about.

This has been a very brief overview of religious reincarnation beliefs as they have developed over untold millennia. As you can see, there have been many ways that reincarnation has been defined. But this book is written from the vantage point of past-life regressions, not theories about reincarnation. As a past-life therapist and researcher, I see a very different picture, one that does not seem to reflect any of the old ideas or beliefs very well. Furthermore, those beliefs have all been tied to religious systems. In our modern time, we may see things from a psychological point of view more than from a religious one. In any case, past-life regression as we know it today, and the past-life therapy that flows from it, shows us dimensions of ourselves that we now identify as psychological. Some people do find a religious component, or at least a spiritual one, but others do not. If you are interested in this field, it is a good idea to know something about the religious systems of reincarnation, but this book is about the healing power and the psychological aspects of past-life regression and therapy, not the religious meanings that might be there. It is about who you are, and who I am, and how we got so different and so much the same.

CHAPTER TWO

A BRIEF OVERVIEW OF PSYCHOLOGY

This chapter presents a brief overview of some theories of psychology and methods of psychotherapy that seem to be relevant to past-life therapy. It is by no means a thorough history of all the theories of psychology and psychotherapy that have developed during the century since Freud, but instead focuses on those that seem to be reflected or not by what we see in past-life regressions. Some readers may find this material unimportant to them, and they can skip the chapter; it is not essential for understanding the later chapters. But some will find the material in this chapter interesting, and for them it may be very relevant to the later chapters.

I must first call attention to the difference between psychology and psychotherapy. Strictly speaking, psychology is the study of people and their feelings, thoughts, and actions; psychotherapy is the attempt to use the discoveries of psychology to help people to function better.

Although today there are innumerable systems of psychotherapy, they can be seen to flow mainly from one of three major categories of psychological theory: analysis, behaviorism, and humanistic psychology. In this chapter I present brief descriptions of those three categories and some of the psychotherapies that flow from them.

ANALYSIS

From 1900 on, three giants, contemporaries of each other—Sigmund Freud, Karl Jung, and Alfred Adler—developed the earliest psychological theories about how the mind works and how we develop. They all developed psychotherapies that are called one or another form of "analysis."

Sigmund Freud and Psychoanalysis

Freud's "psychoanalysis" was based upon his belief that the human mind contained three important levels: the unconscious, the preconscious, and the conscious. According to Freud, the unconscious is the part of the mind of which we are completely unaware; the preconscious is the part that is easily accessible to us; and the conscious, of course, is the part of our mind that we are using at a given moment. For example, as you read these words, your conscious mind is concentrating on what you read, but if I suddenly suggest that you think of your street address, it is right there, available to you: It was tucked into your preconscious all along, ready for you to find and shift into your conscious mind when you want it. The material in your unconscious, however, is not easy to find, and in fact, Freud believed it could not be found at all without psychoanalysis, his "talking cure."

Later, in the 1920s, Freud presented another three-tiered organization of the mind. This was the familiar id, ego, and superego system, and it meshes with his earlier theory. In this system, the id is primitive and inborn; it is what every newborn infant has. The id has no sense of right or wrong. It is packed with instincts and operates from what Freud called the "pleasure principle": the desire to find pleasure and avoid pain. The infant is not born with an ego or a superego; these develop after birth. The ego can be said to be the sense of one's self as an individual, and starts to develop as the infant interacts with others and with his or her environment. The superego begins to develop a bit later, and is learned from parents and others, as the child learns ethical values: what the family and the wider world consider to be "right" and "wrong."

Freud was revolutionary in that he was the first to suggest that there is an unconscious part of the mind that controls our thoughts, actions, and beliefs. This idea is borne out by past-life therapy, in which that very part of the mind seems to be accessed in the process of recalling a past life. On the other hand, Freud constructed numerous other theories, particularly about the processes of gender identification that all children go through, but these theories are not supported by what we see in past-life therapy.

Karl Jung and Analytical Psychotherapy

Karl Jung was an early contemporary of Freud's, and he was at first a friend and follower of Freud's but then parted from him. Jung was already interested in the workings of the unconscious when he met Freud, and he had done some experiments that seemed to support Freud's theories about the existence of the unconscious. Eventually, however, Jung devised a system very different from Freud's.

Both Jung and Freud were interested in dreams and in what they showed us about the unconscious, and each devised a system for interpreting them. But Jung based large parts of his theories on the world's mythology and religious beliefs as well as on dreams. In Jungian psychotherapy, it is only through mythology, dreams, and fantasy that the unconscious can be found.

Like Freud, Jung considered the "psyche" as being subdivided into three parts, but the parts are somewhat different: the ego, the personal unconscious, and the collective (also called nonpersonal) unconscious. These three levels of the psyche interact to create the personality. Jung's ego and personal unconscious share many of the characteristics of Freud's ego and unconscious, but the collective unconscious is distinctly Jung's idea and is most relevant to past-life therapy.

Jung's collective unconscious consists of what he called "archetypes," mythical figures that all people share and that have become embedded in everyone's unconscious over millennia of human history, mythology, and religion. According to Jung, archetypes are inborn in us all. Some examples of archetypes are the Hero, the Great Mother, the Wise Old Man, the Divine Child, God. Ideas also are part of the collective unconscious, such as the idea of rebirth. Certain archetypes play an important role in the development of personality. Especially important ones are the shadow, the *persona*, the *anima/animus*, and the Self.

Briefly, shadow archetypes represent the unacceptable parts of ourselves that we deny; in the process of denial, we bend over backward to be the opposite of the shadow archetype. This can go either way. A person with deeply repressed hostility toward others may seem on the surface to be (and believe himself to be) a friendly, helpful, loving person. On the other hand, a self-effacing, timid person with very low self-esteem may be repressing a healthy shadow that is capable and assertive. In the case of the shadow archetype, this is not mere acting on these people's parts; they truly do not know they have this shadow side, good or bad.

The *persona* archetype is an actor, in a good sense. It is the power of adaptation to circumstances. The *persona* is not so deeply buried as some other archetypes; we all know we act and even feel differently in different circumstances. For example, we act and feel differently at a funeral than at a baseball game or a wedding, and in these cases we know we are doing it. It is only when this archetype is repressed that we get into trouble; many people refuse to admit that they have the ability to change the way they act or feel, to adapt to a change in circumstances.

The *anima* and *animus* archetypes may be truly unconscious archetypes for most people. Jung defined them as representing those parts of ourselves that contain characteristics of the gender opposite to our own. Many modern Jungians, however, believe that each of us has them both. The *anima* tells us what females are like, the *animus*, what males are like. These archetypes not only impel us to behave in certain ways that we have been taught are appropriate for our own gender, they also structure what we expect others to be like, both people of our own gender and those of the opposite one. These archetypes can have very serious effects upon our relationships, because if people don't behave as we think they "should" the relationship will not go well. Furthermore, if we find ourselves wanting to do something that we think is only appropriate for the other gender, we may worry about our own nature as healthy men or women. These two archetypes are the focus of much Jungian therapy today, and it is easy to see why, when our old concepts of "appropriate behavior" for the two genders are changing so fast.

The Self archetype is capitalized in Jungian writings, because it is considered so important. Reaching it is the true goal of therapy and, to a Jungian, of life as well. It represents the whole person, one who has found meaning in life, who has found his or her own unique way, or true "journey." To reach this goal one must free oneself from the compelling power of the other archetypes and become a true individual; the process of doing so is called "individuation." If it is successful, the Self—the "whole" person—emerges.

Unlike Freud, who was a rationalist through and through and had no belief in the "occult," Jung was interested in psychic phenomena, Eastern religious thought, and concepts that are still considered "mystical." He also had an interest in reincarnation; the idea of rebirth is one of the archetypes.

Jung's theories about the collective unconscious are very relevant to past-life therapy as it is practiced today. Many past-life therapists come from Jungian backgrounds in their training, and use past-life stories as they would use dreams in more conventional Jungian psychotherapy, looking for archetypes and connecting them with the person's problems. Some see the collective unconscious as a reality in which all possible archetypes exist, and the person relating a past-life story draws upon it to find the elements most relevant to their particular problems and concerns.

Alfred Adler and Adlerian Analysis

Another contemporary of Freud, and like Jung an early colleague, was Alfred Adler. Also like Jung, Adler developed his theories by building on Freud's work. But there are important differences between Adler's theories and either Jung's or Freud's. Adler came to feel that all human personality is constructed through a person's interactions with others, and these will be different for each person.

According to Adler, although we are born with certain basic hereditary tendencies, these are more positive than negative. At birth, these tendencies begin to be strongly shaped by our environment. How we are treated by parents, siblings, teachers, friends, even strangers, as well as all the things we are taught or learn on our own shape our developing selves in all ways. Basically, for Adler, we begin at birth to shape ourselves in response to all these influences, and continue to do so all our lives.

For Adler, the sense of personal power to make choices and to carry them through is fundamental for a healthy personality. Because people growing up in a complex society are exposed to so many different and often conflicting ways to be, people develop a certain ability to choose their actions and goals. They may choose productive, socially beneficial actions, or harmful, even criminal, ones.

Adler believed that life itself presents us with "life tasks." He stressed three of these tasks: society, work, and sex. We must accept that we are social beings who must interact cooperatively with others; we must find productive work to do; and finally, we must learn to define our sex roles and to relate appropriately to others in our expression of our sexual drives.

Building upon Adler's theories, two other life tasks have recently been suggested by others: acknowledging our spiritual needs, and coming to terms with ourselves. In other words, we must honor our need to define the nature of the universe and our place in it, and we must find a satisfactory balance among the "me, myself, and I" that are parts of us all. Religious impulse as well as scientific curiosity flow from the drive toward accomplishing the first task; our self-questioning nature and sense of unique self-identity flow from the drive toward accomplishing the second.

One of Adler's most important concepts was his belief that people are whole beings, and that the "parts" in Freud's and Jung's theories cannot be examined in isolation. Since all elements of a person interact with all of the others and with the environment, and since this process continues throughout life, a person is constantly changing him- or herself. Adler rejected the primary importance of the "unconscious," considering this as simply those elements of the personality that are not yet understood. Although like Freud and Jung, he considered dreams as coming from the "unconscious" and as important in understanding ourselves, to Adler dreams were most helpful in solving problems. He called dreams "the factory of the emotions." According to him, dreams set our moods for the next day; our dreams can impel us toward an action or away from one.

The goal of Adlerian analysis, the form of psychotherapy based upon Adler's ideas, is to reeducate the client by enlarging his or her awareness of having choices. "Basic mistakes" must be recognized for what they are; basic mistakes can be identified by flat-footed and exaggerated statements like "I never have any luck" or "Nobody cares about me." To Adlerian therapists, it is essential to challenge these basic mistakes.

Of these three pioneers in psychological theory, it is possible that Adler's theories have traveled best and most widely into our own time, although Jungian therapy is much used today. But a good many of Adler's theories have become the foundation stones for modern theories and psychotherapies, although too often he is not given the credit he deserves. All forms of social psychology, for example, or Gestalt psychology, or any other which stresses the importance of interactions between people, can be traced to his similar ideas. Our modern ideas of healthy child-rearing reflect the importance of early experiences with parents, siblings, and the wider environment. Many of his theories and psychotherapy methods have moved straight into cognitive therapy. And his perception of the holistic nature of human beings has been the foundation of humanistic psychology and of our more spiritually oriented psychotherapies and theories, such as transpersonal psychology and past-life therapy.

Jung's theories, too, have had their impact on the development of modern therapies, especially his theories of the *anima/animus* and the shadow archetypes, which have proven very useful in psychotherapy. And both Jung's and Adler's concepts of the individuating, always-changing Self are basic to humanistic and transpersonal psychotherapies and to past life therapy as well.

BEHAVIORISM

The roots of behaviorism go back to the mid-1800s. In the 1860s, Ivan Sechenov, a Russian physiologist, concluded from his studies of the brain that all behavior stemmed from the organism's responses to stimulation. Based upon Sechenov's findings, Ivan Pavlov devised his famous experiments on dogs. Pavlov noted that the dogs' natural response to eating or smelling food (the stimulus) was to salivate (the response). He at first rang a bell every time the dogs were fed; then he rang the bell just before they were fed, and finally rang it at odd times of day, without feeding them immediately afterward. The dogs began to salivate whenever they heard the bell, whether there was food present or not. They had come to associate the sound of the bell with food and salivated in response. Since there was no food or smell of food present that would physically stimulate salivation, this association of the bell with food must have taken place in their brains.

In 1920, John B. Watson and Rosalie Rayner created a phobia for white furry objects in a small child by making a loud unpleasant noise that frightened the child whenever he saw a white rat in a cage. This is similar to what Pavlov had achieved with dogs almost a century earlier. The child became phobic for other white animals, both real and toy. This, so far as is known, was the first time behavioral techniques were deliberately used with a human being. Such an experiment would be considered unethical today, but Watson and Rayner did demonstrate the powers of behavioral techniques with children.

Behaviorism is often thought to explain "how" we learn. Most basically, and simplistically, we learn the way Pavlov's dogs did. Being human, our levels of learning are more complicated, and what we learn is mediated by our minds, but like the dogs, we learn to associate certain stimuli with rewards or punishments and respond accordingly.

Perhaps the two men most influential in shaping modern American behaviorism were Joseph Wolpe and B. F. Skinner. In the mid-1950s, Skinner and his followers found that behavior could be changed by means of what they called conditioning; that is, repeatedly associating good or bad results with various actions. For example, if someone is given an electric shock every time he or she pushes a red button, the person will quickly learn not to push that button, and may develop a fear of it. On the other hand, if the person is given a reward every time the red button is pushed, he or she will push the red button frequently.

This is actually the basis for all the punishments or praise that all parents have always used to get their children to behave as the parents want. With human beings, words and gestures from important people function as punishments and rewards just as effectively as blows or pieces of candy. A growing child learns early which actions are rewarded with a smile (or a piece of candy) and which are punished with a frown and a "No" (or a spanking).

In all of this one should not define the word "action" too narrowly. In behaviorist theory, actions need not be physical actions: Thoughts, attitudes, and even feelings are "actions." Thus, many a boy child is scorned and called a sissy (punishment) if he cries when hurt, whereas if he does not cry, he is praised as a "brave boy" (reward). It doesn't take much of this to teach the boy that boys (and men) do not cry when hurt, and that "real men" are brave. The boy has been conditioned to this belief and will act accordingly.

In this way, according to behaviorists, we learn all of our attitudes and beliefs, and we also learn how to express them fittingly. Furthermore, Skinner and his followers found that by substituting punishment for rewards (or vice versa) for a given behavior, the behavior can be changed.

Skinner has been much criticized because he advocated deliberately applying the theories of behaviorism to the larger community. Having high ethical standards himself, Skinner saw a benign society as the desired goal, but the unpleasant phrase "social engineering" also comes from this idea. We are actually on a slippery slope here. It is probably true that all societies condition their members to certain behavior, beliefs, and attitudes, and although this usually occurs naturally and not deliberately, it can also be done with purpose. And that purpose may not be what we would call a good one.

Hitler comes to mind here. He used behaviorist principles, too, although probably inadvertently. He rewarded or punished those who were either willing or unwilling to go along with his genocidal laws. Our recent history tells us how tragically successful he was.

What is most relevant here is that a good many people, exposed to the constant barrage of Hitler's propaganda, rewards for obedience, and the certainty of severe punishment for disobedience, obeyed the powers that be. But it is also relevant, and equally important, that there were others who did not, despite the risk to their own lives, and they show us the limits of this kind of conditioning when it contradicts the ethical standards already developed in a human mind. This was behavioral social engineering with a vengeance, but it was not total, and perhaps in a pluralistic society it can never be total.

Yet all societies teach their children the values of the society, and this is done, essentially, by rewards and punishments, just as

Skinner said. And in any society, those approved values tend to be those that keep the society going smoothly along. This is perhaps one of the best arguments in favor of a pluralistic society with democratic traditions, in which people from many different backgrounds have many different values but still manage to get along with each other fairly well. In democracies, the "getting along" part is one of the most important values that is taught.

In 1958, Joseph Wolpe presented a theory that has become the basis for much behavior therapy. He held that anxiety (fear responses) could not be maintained when the organism was physically relaxed because anxiety required physical tension. Wolpe developed what is called systematic desensitization, a method of teaching people to relax while they think of or are in the presence of a feared object. This treatment is much used today in the treatment of phobias, and has proven successful. It is usually carried out in the therapist's office at first, but eventually the person will learn to use the techniques wherever they seem necessary.

There have been many variants on Wolpe's approach, and one could say it is the basis of all the relaxation therapies that flourish today, and not just for phobias. People have many fears: fears of relationships, actions, even accomplishments. Since physical relaxation by definition reduces physical tension, it will reduce the anxiety a person might feel when even thinking about the feared situation.

What we see in past-life therapy reflects some of the basic ideas of conditioning as presented in behaviorist theory. We "learn" to fear water, for example, because of one or more negative experiences with water in one or more of our past lives. We may have drowned in a recent past life, and this experience has been carried forward into our present life as a fear of water. Thus we have been "conditioned" to fear water. And examining the experience in hypnosis, a very relaxed state, helps us to be free of the fear.

COGNITIVE PSYCHOLOGY

The theorists of cognitive psychology go beyond behaviorism to note that humans have minds that mediate a person's responses to conditioning. In the 1950s, Albert Ellis developed what he called

Rational-Emotive Therapy (RET) and William Glaser developed what he called Reality Therapy. Aaron Beck extended these in the 1970s into what is now called Cognitive Psychology.

Ellis held that although animals may respond predictably to stimuli, people have minds and interpret events according to their belief systems and those belief systems will moderate their responses to stimuli. By "belief systems," Ellis meant beliefs about the world in general. They are acquired in childhood, and they are collections of largely unrecognized assumptions about the world. We see this moderation by belief systems happening in the example I gave of the people who resisted Hitler's propaganda. His propaganda violated their ethical belief systems, and they refused to act as Hitler was trying to condition them to act.

Ellis believed that all people are born with the ability to be both rational and irrational, to think, feel, and act in either self-actualizing or self-defeating ways. Although thinking, feeling, and acting interact and influence each other, the way one thinks determines the ways one feels and acts and is the key to change and growth. Ellis developed RET to challenge the person's irrational thinking processes. He had little patience with long excursions into the person's childhood looking for insight. To Ellis, what mattered was to change the thinking and thus the behavior in the here and now no matter where it started.

Reality Therapy was developed by William Glaser in the 1950s. Glaser advocated using the challenging approach, but not always the methods, of RET in identifying and changing clients' irrational beliefs, and he had no patience with "excuses" for dysfunctional behavior. He believed that every individual must take full responsibility for his or her behavior in the present, no matter what unpleasant experiences may have occurred in the past. For him, the here and now and the future were the important things, and dredging up old past experiences, even traumatic ones, had no place in his therapy.

Glaser refused to place psychiatric labels on clients. What are called mental illnesses in other psychotherapy systems are considered irresponsibility in Reality Therapy, and clients are assumed to be trying their best to find their identity in whatever ways they know. Reality Therapy tries to help clients accept responsibility for their actions and to develop a "success identity" by focusing on the here and now and on what the client plans to do next. Glaser considered that no one was a helpless victim of his or her past; people always choose their own actions whether they admit it or not. If they choose to be a victim of the past and deny responsibility, they are creating a "failure identity."

In the 1970s, Aaron Beck developed Cognitive Therapy, treatment methods based partly on Ellis's and Glaser's principles but extending them. Many of Beck's methods have proven effective, and today most therapists of all kinds use some of them, even past-life therapists. The basic idea is to first ascertain what the client's irrational beliefs are; this can often be gleaned from the statements of the client, such as "I fail at everything I try." This is a clear statement of an irrational and untrue belief held by the client. (It is what Adler called a "basic mistake.") The statement is too sweeping: Like all of us, the client fails at some things and succeeds at others.

The first step, for the cognitive therapist, would be to point this out to the client and ask him or her to name some things at which he or she has *not* failed. The client will say there is nothing; the therapist may have to start by pointing out that the client managed successfully to make an appointment with the therapist and get to the office, perhaps even on time. The client will deny that this amounts to anything important, but it does weaken the all-or-nothing, irrational nature of "I fail at everything I try." The client has not failed in getting to the therapy session. He can only honestly say, "I fail at some things I try," and since this is the common experience of human beings, it is much less devastating.

In Cognitive Therapy, the next steps are to find out from the client what kinds of things he really does fail at, why this bothers him, and what he thinks might be stopping him, then work out a plan of action to test his ideas and eventually try one of the failure activities and succeed at it. This therapy focuses upon the thoughts, ideas, and actions of the client, and homework is important.

In RET, Reality Therapy, and Cognitive Therapy, feelings, both pleasant and unpleasant ones, are thought to come from thoughts, not the other way around. Someone who complains that "I fail at everything I try" has an underlying thought, a "belief," that "failure is shameful," and he or she will naturally feel frightened at the idea of trying anything that might result in failure and shame. In this way his feelings of anxiety and fear are born, but his thought that "failure is shameful" comes first.

Behavior and cognitive therapies have been tested by research and have demonstrated some success as therapies. To these therapists, long sessions spent gaining insight into the "roots" of problems may be a waste of time. Behavior and cognitive therapies are focused as much as possible upon the specific problems the person comes to therapy for, deal with those problems in a straightforward manner, and take many fewer sessions than analytical therapies.

Past-life therapy contradicts the focus on the here and now that characterizes these forms of therapy. After all, in past-life therapy, one does "go back into the past" to find the roots of problems, and often very far back into the past.

But the idea of the mind and its beliefs shaping the emotions is supported. What one finds in past-life therapy is that one made a *decision:* for example, that water is frightening, and it is this decision that is carried forward into subsequent lives as a belief. Although to a person with a phobia for water, their fear reaction may seem irrational and entirely emotional, in past-life therapy we find that the irrational emotion of fear stems from that old decision, a belief that they formed about water long ago as a direct result of an unpleasant experience in a past life, perhaps drowning. In this context, the fear becomes rational. This extremely unpleasant experience has conditioned them to fear water and they made a decision that "water is frightening," and they bring that old decision forward as a belief into their present life.

Humanistic Psychology

Abraham Maslow is usually considered the father of humanistic psychology, although many strains have led into it; indeed, it reaches back to Adler. In the 1960s, Maslow developed most fully Adler's concept of the self-actualizing person. He believed that everyone was born with a desire to actualize his or her potentials for creativity, love, meaningful work, social conscience, and meaningful relationships.

Maslow was especially interested in the healthy person, as opposed to the mentally ill person. He asked: What makes a person mentally healthy? Maslow believed the healthy person is naturally curious and continues to grow and develop throughout his or her life: to self-actualize. When this does not occur, Maslow believed it was because some "basic need" had not been met early in life. The basic needs are for food, security, and love, and they start to be satisfied or not at birth. If these needs are not met, the person will not progress to the self-actualizing needs above, or not without therapy. Maslow, like Glaser and Adler before him, placed great importance on personal responsibility and socially "right" action, action that is moral and that will be constructive, rather than destructive, for society at large.

Humanistic psychology uses forms of therapy based on Carl Rogers's ideas. Rogers began to develop his theories in the 1940s, and was one of the major forerunners and developers of humanistic psychotherapy. Rogers held that the therapist should give the client accepting, nonjudgmental "unconditional positive regard." The therapist listens and "reflects" the value of the client; whatever the client says is true for the client, and that's what needs to be accepted. In fact, in the 1970s Rogers rejected the word "client"; he had previously called his method "client-centered therapy," but in 1974 he changed this to "person-centered therapy." Therapy is centered upon the client as a *person* who is trying to become self-actualizing in his or her own best ways, and the therapist's task is to help him or her to do this.

The methods of humanistic psychotherapy tend to be much more oriented toward examining the past than behaviorism or RET, Reality Therapy, or Cognitive Therapy. In fact, it was partly the belief that these approaches were too limited to deal with the whole person that gave rise to humanistic psychology. So it was that with humanistic psychology, psychotherapy came back around to some of the older theories and methods of Freud, Jung, and Adler, with their emphasis upon the unconscious and the Self, and on the need for insight and understanding of oneself.

William James is also often considered one of the fathers of humanistic psychology; in the early 1900s, he insisted upon the importance of the subjective, introspective approach to self-understanding. His ideas have become part of the methods of humanistic psychotherapy, which encourages honest introspection as a way to become aware of one's true motivations, fears, and goals.

A good many psychologists and therapists call themselves humanistic today, including some behaviorist and cognitive psychotherapists. This is because the primary goal of humanistic psychotherapy, the idea of the self-actualizing person, is ultimately the same goal all therapists try to help their clients reach, whatever methods they use.

One of Maslow's self-actualizing needs was that people have a spiritual need to find a meaning in their lives that transcends their daily lives. This need has traditionally been met by religious belief but can be met by other spiritual beliefs, such as a personal awareness of being a part of humanity as a whole. These ideas have led to transpersonal psychology.

TRANSPERSONAL PSYCHOLOGY

Transpersonal psychology grew in part from humanistic psychology, and like it, it is also a reaction against the apparent limitations of other therapies. Transpersonal therapies are still being developed, but in general, they incorporate Jung's idea of people's need to individuate, Adler's stress on personal responsibility, Maslow's concepts of self-actualization and spiritual needs, and James' subjective, introspective methods. In transpersonal psychology, people are encouraged to get past their narrow ego identifications and identify themselves as part of the larger human enterprise. The subjective, inner experience is all-important; various mind-altering methods are cultivated to reach a sense of oneness with others, with God, and with the universe itself. In the 1960s and 1970s, drugs were sometimes used for this, but today this is rare and it is more usual to use meditation or guided altered-state techniques.

Transpersonal psychology takes the experience of the person as real, valid, and important for the person no matter how unusual or "weird" the experience might be. These experiences include psychic phenomena such as psychic dreams, out-of-body experiences, past-life flashbacks, and mystical states. Most other forms of psychology have considered such experiences as illusions, hallucinations, or evidence of serious mental problems. Transpersonal psychotherapists accept these experiences as being as real and valid for the person reporting them as any other experience, and not necessarily as a symptom of some dire problem.

In fact, a new concept in transpersonal psychology, that of "spiritual emergence," has been developed by Stanislav Grof. Grof holds that psychic phenomena and transcendent experiences are a sign of spiritual growth of the highest order, and should be encouraged and learned from. He and other transpersonal psychologists believe that, through these experiences, people can truly leave behind their narrow personal identifications and recognize their true place in the universe as spiritual planetary citizens.

Transpersonal psychology, like humanistic psychology, starts with the idea that people are basically healthy and self-actualizing, a radical difference from Freud and Jung and from behavior and cognitive psychology. Until the development of humanistic psychology, the focus of psychology was on the sickness of the person. Maslow insisted that psychology should notice the basic healthy impulses of people, the drive toward self-actualization, and build on that. Transpersonal psychology takes the spiritual need as a healthy one, and builds on that.

POSTMODERN PSYCHOLOGY

A new and still developing approach in psychology today is postmodern psychology, and like transpersonal psychology, it has yet to be fully defined. But it has arisen from the recognition, forced upon us by our modern global awareness, that people have many different ways to be in their many different cultures. One of the ideas of postmodern psychology is that people are born able to learn whatever roles and beliefs their particular culture expects of them, and once having learned these roles and beliefs, they tend to believe that their culture's way is the best and right one for everyone.

No structured form of psychotherapy has developed based on these ideas yet, although some multinational corporations, as well as the Peace Corps, now provide workshops for people who are about to move into a new and different culture, to prepare them for the often very different cultural beliefs and behaviors they will find, some of them shocking and disturbing to the Western mind. And it is possible that past-life therapy may turn out to be the form of therapy that fits best with the ideas of postmodern psychology, because of the picture it gives us of ourselves as spiritual beings and as very adaptable "citizens of the planet."

OTHER PSYCHOTHERAPIES

Most other psychotherapies today fit within one or the other of the frameworks above, except for postmodern psychology, which has developed no specific form of therapy yet. There are many variants of all of the psychotherapies above, but if you look at the theories behind them and the therapy methods used, they can be seen to stem from one or another of the major theories, or mixtures of them.

For example, Transactional Analysis, a popular form of therapy today, takes a cognitive approach to Freud's idea of the id, ego, and superego; Gestalt therapy, another popular therapy, is based upon Adler's ideas of the importance of one's interactions with others. Variants of Jungian therapy are flourishing, and their examination of the various archetypes is very relevant to the changing roles our modern time thrusts upon us. Group therapies are very common today, and can be seen to stem from Adler's insistence upon the importance of social interactions; family therapy deals with those interactions within the family, and other group therapies deal with other social interactions.

CONCLUSION

As you see, there are a good many approaches to psychology and psychotherapy that have developed during the past century. Many theories and therapies have been developed and they have all had their successes. Today, most psychotherapists use combinations of therapies that seem most suitable for the client at hand. One newcomer, of course, is past-life therapy, the subject of this book. I discuss its development in the next chapter. But as we proceed through this book, some readers might like to consider the various theories of the other forms of psychology discussed in this chapter and notice in what ways the past lives discussed support or contradict them. I discuss the most obvious when they arise, but others are also sometimes relevant.

In the next chapter I present an overview of past-life therapy as it has developed over the last three decades.

CHAPTER THREE

A BRIEF OVERVIEW OF PAST-LIFE REGRESSION

The phrase "past-life regression" is used in many ways. Sometimes a so-called psychic, or channeler, claims to go into an altered state of consciousness and "read" other people's past lives for them, or they may "read" people's past lives from Tarot cards or crystals or some other focusing device. Some astrologers claim to be able to see a person's past lives in his or her birth chart, and some aura readers claim to see people's past lives in their auras. So-called past-life regressions are sometimes elicited by massage therapy, or by Reiki techniques.

These practitioners claim to achieve what they call "past-life regression," but this is not the kind of regression discussed in this book, nor is it usually called past-life *therapy*, nor are such readings always accurate. I have worked with clients who have been to psychics or channelers and who later came to me because they wanted to experience in hypnosis the wondrous lives these channelers described to them. However, under hypnosis they were completely unable to "reach" those lives but did access other past lives. Since the past lives that they actually reported in hypnosis were invariably less glorious than the psychics' visions (no priestess in Atlantis, no architect of pyramids), those clients were sometimes very disappointed. But the simpler, more ordinary lives had come from their *own* minds in hypnosis, not the psychic's mind and not mine.

As a hypnotherapist, I have used hypnosis to access past lives for over twenty years. These hypnotically facilitated regressions are the kinds discussed in this book. In the middle of the nineteenth century, early hypnotists, called "magnetizers" at that time, discovered that people in hypnosis sometimes reported lives that they claimed to have lived before. At first, some psychical researchers considered these past-life stories to be a possible way to "prove" that reincarnation really happens. However, they found that some of the details people gave were not always found in the records where they should be found if the past life was a real one. In our scientific age, it was easy to conclude that such stories were imagination at work, and although a few researchers continued to examine them as curiosities, there wasn't much interest in them for any other reason.

In 1956 there was a brief flurry of interest when amateur hypnotist Morey Bernstein published *The Search for Bridey Murphy*, in which he described in great detail the six hypnotic regression sessions he held with an American woman who related the life of "Bridey Murphy," an Irish woman of the nineteenth century. This book became immediately popular and eventually became the basis for a play and a movie, and it inspired journalists and historians to investigate the factual material the woman gave. Some of this was found to be accurate, some inaccurate, and some was not traceable at all. Meanwhile, many mental health professionals on both sides of the Atlantic panned the book. They claimed that it was dangerous to elicit these "past lives" and that they were all fantasies; this was "obvious" to them. Thanks partly to this treatment by the mental health establishment, interest in past-life regression continued at a low ebb for another twenty years, until the mid-1970s.

One reason for this lack of interest was that past-life regressions seemed to have no practical use. Past-life stories were curiosities, nothing more. There had been one or two therapists in Great Britain who had used them in therapy over the years, particularly Arnoll Bloxham in Wales and Denys Kelsey in England, but they published little and attracted scant and mostly scathing attention from other professionals.

Then, in the mid-1970s, some enterprising therapists discovered that whether fantasies or real, these past-life stories were sometimes almost miraculously effective in psychotherapy. By the end of the

1970s, several books by therapists discussing their own cases and one reporting a research project were available to therapists, and more and more therapists were reading them and trying out this new and rapid way to help their clients. Most regressions today are individual, for purposes of therapy. But there are many regression sessions scheduled because of simple curiosity, and group workshops for this purpose are more popular every year.

In 1980, the Association for Past Life Research and Therapies was formed in California under the guidance of Dr. Hazel Denning, a psychologist who had been quietly using past-life regressions in therapy since the 1960s. This organization still flourishes today under its new name, the International Association for Regression Research and Therapies (IARRT) and with nearly a thousand members in over twenty countries. It functions as an international clearing house for the field, with a bookstore, a quarterly newsletter, a juried journal, conferences twice a year, and a website. Both laypeople and professionals belong, with a steadily increasing membership among mental health professionals.

There has been some research in past life regressions, although not nearly enough. Dr. Helen Wambach, in 1978, published the results of a study she carried out in group workshop settings with normal, healthy people. Altogether, she examined over a thousand past-life stories, and found that the details of everyday life that the people reported, even obscure details, were almost all accurate and that the demographic breakdown for the times and places they reported having lived in was consistent with known historical fact.

Wambach and Dr. Chet Snow, in 1986, did another study in which they examined the experience of 26 past-life therapists and what their clients reported. Dr. Rabia Clark, in 1995, did a larger survey, of 136 therapists, and gathered a great deal of information about how past-life therapy is practiced in the United States today.

In 1993, Robert James, using individual sessions, found that of 104 normal, healthy people in deep hypnosis, 81 were able to report at least one past life. In 1995, James repeated his study, this time with 44 people, with similar results. In the second study, James asked for the people's most recent lifetimes, and when those were in the United States, he asked for details such as names, dates and places of birth and death, and other details that could be checked in census and other records. James is still checking these records; it is a big job.

In 1995, I myself carried out a research study in which I worked with 37 people with phobias of various kinds. The therapeutic results of examining the past lives were excellent and "statistically significant," as the scientists say. I also found significant patterns in the numbers of past lives they reported and the kinds of past-life or interlife experiences they said had caused the phobias.

In a very small previous study, in 1982, I worked with two women and attempted to examine the differences between what they reported when I directed them into a "fantasy" and into a "past life," and found many differences. For one thing, they could easily change things like colors or kinds of food in their fantasies, but it was difficult and sometimes impossible to make such changes in their past lives. One of the women commented that after making a change in a past life, if she looked away and then back again, the item "snapped back" to its prior state. Furthermore, neither one was able to "fantasize a past life" when directed to do so in hypnosis; only when I directed them to actually "go back into one of your past lives" did they produce a past life.

In a study carried out in 1995 by Ronald van der Maesen in the Netherlands, 8 out of 10 people with Tourette's Syndrome improved by means of past life therapy. These results were based upon a one-year's follow-up questionnaire, and were just released in English in 1998.

In 1999, van der Maesen published a second study of the effectiveness of past-life therapy with the hallucinated voices that schizophrenics sometimes hear. Of 27 volunteers, at six-month follow-up 52% indicated that past life therapy alleviated the hearing of hallucinated voices; four reported that the voices had ceased entirely. 78% said that the therapy had had other important and positive meanings for them.

Dr. Ian Stevenson has carried out research that, while not with past-life regressions per se, does involve the possibility of reincarnation. Since the 1960s, Stevenson has investigated the stories of hundreds of young children who spontaneously speak of their prior lives; many of these are in countries other than the United States. Carol Bowman, in 1995, gathered a great number of cases of

American children like this. I discuss Stevenson's and Bowman's findings in more detail in Chapter 11.

A number of therapists have attempted to trace the details given in individual past-life regressions to see if they are accurate. These attempts are more or less successful. Hypnotherapist Rick Brown and psychologist Dr. Linda Tarazi have each published a very successful attempt of this kind.

Both of them found, after much searching, that the factual material their clients gave, such as names, dates, and descriptions of places and events, were accurate. What is especially interesting about their studies is that the details were not easy to find; both had to trace old records that had been undisturbed for decades in Brown's case, centuries in Tarazi's. Tarazi, in fact, had to travel to Spain and the Caribbean and employ a translator to translate the centuries-old church documents she had to examine.

As you can see from the above, although some research has been carried out, most of it is sparse and depends upon the interests and resources of the individual researcher. But as the field of past-life therapy grows, more research will certainly be carried out.

When discussing this subject, it is always wise to be sure that everyone is talking about the same things, and that the words and concepts used are understood. Since past-life regression and past-life therapy are fairly new, and since there are various methods that are said to reach a past life, I will define some terms and describe some of these methods below. A good many techniques have been developed for accessing and using past-life regressions in therapy and in workshop settings. There are, however, certain features that are common to all hypnotic regressions to past lives. The basics are:

1. The person (or people, in a workshop) is guided by the therapist into hypnosis. Best results seem to come from a medium-to-deep level of hypnosis, and although every past-life therapist has his or her own favorite methods, they all use some form of hypnosis induction, although they may not call it that. This usually involves deep relaxation with the eyes closed and the use of guided imagery by imagining some calm scene, such as a beach or a woodland setting. By simply watching, an experienced hypnotherapist can usually tell approximately what level of hypnosis you have

reached, but there are also various quick and unobtrusive tests to measure your level. Well-trained hypnotherapists are experienced with these tests and most use them sometimes, and some use them always.

It is possible that if you are at a light trance level you might report a past life, but I have learned through my own experience that these light-trance stories are different in many ways from a deeper-level past-life narrative, and are probably fantasies. It seems strange to put it this way, but one could say that in a light trance people actually know too much. They tend to be excited, speak fluently and clearly, volunteer all the names and dates and have a "bird's-eye view" of the whole life right from the start of the regression. They volunteer sweeping information about where and when the life is taking place, and know all about the larger political situation and the general social conditions of the time and place. There is a lot of excitement but little real emotion shown, and little connection with any of their present-day problems or concerns. Furthermore, the past-life character is often someone who can be found in history books.

Past-life stories that come from the deeper levels of hypnosis are very different. In these, people are almost monosyllabic and may speak inaudibly—I have often given the direct hypnotic suggestion that the person "can speak clearly and easily" so that I could hear them at all. At these deeper levels, you would most likely have trouble knowing your own first name in the past life, let alone any other factual information, you would have no idea "what happens next" until we get there, and until we finish the regression, you would not know where or when that life is taking place. If asked directly during the regression, people will guess, but later, on an imaginary screen, their Upper Mind is apt to name a place and date completely different from their guess. And unfortunately, in this kind of regression, the past-life person is most likely historically obscure.

For these reasons I believe that if you seek to know your past lives from hypnotic regressions, you should be sure that the person you go to is well trained in hypnosis as well as experienced in past-life regression. A well-trained hypnotherapist will help you reach your deepest possible level of hypnosis and explore your past lives most thoroughly, and you are more likely to get the real thing. The methods I describe below apply to what happens when a medium-to-deep hypnosis level is reached.

Another reason to be sure your therapist is well trained in hypnosis is that hypnosis itself can produce various phenomena that may seem strange to the hypnotized person, such as feelings of spinning or floating, or that their body is very large or small or has disappeared entirely or melted into the chair, or something that seems like an out-of-body experience, or hearing voices that seem to come from the great beyond. Most people do not have these experiences, but when they do occur, they can be very frightening. A therapist trained in hypnosis recognizes these for what they are, merely signs that you have reached a very deep level of hypnosis. Such a therapist will reassure you that your experience is perfectly normal and not part of the past-life regression, and can "stabilize" your perceptions back to normal.

2. Once a good hypnosis level is reached, you will be guided back into the past-life memory. A common method is by using an imaginary "vehicle." My own favorite vehicle is a "magic chair," but I sometimes use others, depending upon the client. There are probably as many "vehicles" as there are past-life therapists. I have heard and read of trains, boats, bubbles, birds, clouds, and flying carpets that waft the person into the past life. Some methods call for more energy from the person, such as imagining opening a door or walking through a tunnel, over a bridge, up or down stairs, or through an art gallery; with this last, you would find a picture in the gallery that leads into the past life. Any methods such as these seem to do, although some therapists (and clients) feel more comfortable with one or another. For example, for a person with a phobia for bridges, I would not use the "walking across a bridge" technique. Once the past life is reached, you would be instructed to move out into it.

Some therapists do not use any "vehicle." Instead, they instruct the hypnotized client to "go back to the first time you ever had that feeling" or some such direction. This technique is called the "affect-bridge" technique, and it will sometimes place clients into a past life, but they will usually find themselves in the midst of some traumatic situation that they will not understand but that may be truly terrifying. I myself prefer to use my more manageable and gradual "magic chair" or some other vehicle.

3. As just mentioned, unless they are instructed otherwise, people are apt to move into a past life in the midst of some highly traumatic, stressful event. For this reason, many past-life therapists, including myself, instruct the person before they go back that they will enter the past life on an "ordinary, average, day" or at a "calm, comfortable moment." This gives both you and your therapist a chance to find out some basic things about the past life before moving into any stressful events. It is easy to instruct you to "go to your home" or "go to a mealtime" or some such simple, daily activity, and in the process get a sense of where and who the past-life person is. From these entry moments, you can be guided to "go to the next important thing that happens," or "go back one year," or given similar neutral directions. Most people either see or sense these scenes and can describe them in detail in response to general questions from the therapist. If directed by the therapist, they can move back into their past-life childhood or forward until they find their death.

4. Moving through a death experience in a past-life regression can be smoothly and easily done, if the therapist hypnotically suggests that you will remain calm and have no distress no matter what happens. Then you will "zoom through" quickly and you will usually find yourself hovering over your past-life body. From this vantage point you can then go back into the past life to find the most meaningful events, or the happiest moment, or in therapy, the events connected with whatever problem brought you into therapy, and you can examine these events calmly if instructed to do so. I myself use this "calm" direction to people at the beginning of a regression and continue it throughout.

5. After the death experience you can access the lessons you learned in that lifetime and can become aware of the overall meaning of the lifetime for you. You can also continue your journey after death; most people report "floating" up into brightness, where they may be greeted by other people, also disembodied. This is the "interlife," which I describe more fully in Chapter 12. It is a profound and moving experience for most people.

6. Most therapists will bring you back to the present time and

place by the same vehicle or other means by which the past life was accessed, and you will then be roused from hypnosis. Although early hypnotists gave their subjects posthypnotic suggestions that they would not remember the regression after they woke, today's more modern approach does just the opposite: Most therapists tell people they will remember their regression experience after they wake, and most people do. Before rousing them, I always tell clients that they will be able to remember the experience if they want to, and they always do. Without that instruction, which is a direct hypnotic suggestion, after all, people usually remember the past life after they wake, but in a foggy way, as they might remember a dream. With that suggestion, almost all remember it clearly. But either way, you will remember only those parts of the past life that were examined during the regression. This is one reason to examine a past life thoroughly: so the person can get a good sense of the overall nature of the life as a whole. Clients tend to see many more meaningful and subtle past-life connections with their present lives than I do, if they have explored all the important events of the life, the good and the bad alike, and after the regression they continue to recognize meaningful aspects of it that may have escaped their notice during the past-life experience itself.

Many past-life therapists believe that a client will be healed only if he or she "relives" the traumatic past-life experiences that have caused their problems. For this reason, these therapists place the person in the relevant stressful events fully and with full awareness, insisting that they reexperience all the original physical and emotional distress associated with them. This makes for stressful regressions and sometimes clients decide once is enough. A few therapists, including myself, have found that, for us at least, therapy results are better and faster with a calmer approach, and that in both therapy and workshops people see and remember much more detail. Furthermore, people truly enjoy the experience. That is why I tell people that they will "remain calm and comfortable no matter what happens," and they usually do.

Although past-life regressions are useful in therapy, you should always remember that not all problems are caused by past-life experiences. Many troubles stem entirely from experiences earlier in our lives. Even when past lives are involved, there is usually some "triggering" incident in this present life that sets the problem off. This is usually a trivial event, some minor thing that happened very early in life, of which you probably have no conscious memory. But it acted as a trigger for the past-life events, and set them off like a primed gun waiting to be fired.

In therapy, it is possible to find out quickly whether or not a past life is involved in your problems. One technique that is used by many therapists is to ask the person's "Upper Mind" or "Higher Self" what the sources of the client's problems are. The Upper Mind will indicate whether any past lives are involved or not. A good definition of this part of the mind is "that part of your mind that is wise, knows everything, and wants the best for you." There seems to be some unconscious part of our minds that this description fits, because when fingers are used to indicate "yes" or "no" to a therapist's questions, they seem to rise by themselves in response to questions, or answers will just flow onto an imaginary screen without the client's conscious effort and then the client can read off what is on the screen.

By questioning the Upper Mind, it is possible to find out quickly whether or not any past lives caused the client's problems and, if so, how many past lives were involved and whether it is permissible to examine them. (Sometimes it isn't; the Upper Mind is cautious.) Given this information and permission, the therapist then guides the client in the chosen vehicle or other method calmly back into "an average, ordinary day in whatever past life should be examined first," leaving it up to the Upper Mind to decide the correct order in which the relevant past lives should be examined.

If past lives were not involved, it is possible to use the same regression methods to explore incidents in the client's present life that may have caused the problem. However, since these "real-life" events may be quite traumatic (unlike a triggering event) and may involve family members or people the client still knows in his or her present life, the Upper Mind may protect the client by refusing to examine various events or by setting a slower pace. A wise therapist never pushes, but goes as slowly as necessary, whether past- or present-life events are to be examined.

By these methods, people access a past life in little vignettes, scenes that they "see" very literally but that are usually out of context. The transcript below gives some idea of the visual literalness with which most clients "see" events but at the same time understand little of their overall situation. This client, Betty, has just stepped from her magic chair into a past life. (The name "Betty" is not her real name. All the clients' names I use in this book are fictitious, to protect the clients' anonymity.)

Therapist: . . . looking around; are you outdoors or indoors?

Betty: Outdoors.

T: All right. You're outdoors. Are you standing or sitting?

B: Standing.

T: Okay. Is it countryside or is it a town or a city?

B: I think it's the country.

T: All right. Look down. What kind of ground are you standing on? What kind of terrain is it?

B: Dirt road.

T: It's a dirt road. Okay. Look around on either side of the dirt road. What's the landscape like? [pause] It's interesting as you move on into it.

B: Hills, and a field in front of the hills, and then the dirt road.

T: All right. Do you think it's summer or winter?

B: It's summer.

T: It's summer. Okay. How do you know that?

B: It's green.

T: Mm-hm. Is it a pleasant day?

B: Mm-hm [yes].

T: Okay. Now become aware of yourself, look down at yourself. What are you wearing?

B: Shoes, socks, short pants.

T: Mm-hm. Are you a child or an adult?

B: A child.

T: All right. Do you think you're male or female?

B: Male.

T: So you're a young boy?

B: Mm-hm.

T: About how old are you?

B: Eight or nine.

T: Do you live near there?

B: Mm-hm.

T: Okay. I'm going to ask you to place yourself standing in front of your home now, looking at it. Three-two-one-zero. Okay, you're looking at your home, and you can tell me about it. What's it made of?

B: It's attached to other homes.

T: All right. Like row houses?

B: I don't think it's the country.

T: All right. Well, you started out in the country, but perhaps your home is not in the country. Is that right?

B: That's—that's right.

T: All right. Look around the neighborhood where your house is there. Get an idea—is it a town? a village? a city? Is it large?

B: It's large.

T: It's large—

B: It's a city.

T: It's a city. What kinds of vehicles are there on the roads?

B: Horses, wagons. The street is dirt in part.

T: In part?

B: Parts of it are in dirt.

T: And what about the other part?

B: Stone.

T: Stone. Like cobblestones? Small stones?

B: Flat, big stones.

Betty's short, literal answers are characteristic of many people experiencing a regression at very deep levels of hypnosis. Although it is not evident in the transcript, her answers came slowly, after long pauses. Like most clients, she took several seconds to answer each of my questions, as she focused on the ground or her clothing or whatever I had asked her about. However, focusing on these seemingly unimportant details deepened Betty's level of hypnosis and made it possible for more important details to be seen and recognized as we moved through the past life. This is true for all clients, and most past-life therapists ask for details in this way, especially at the beginning of a regression.

One reason I chose this particular transcript is that I made some mistakes in the exchange, and they show us something about hypnosis and past-life regressions. For one thing, it contains several places where I (carelessly) suggested something specific, but Betty answered me otherwise. For example, in the last exchange, where I suggested that the stones might be "Like cobblestones? Small stones?" she answered, "Flat, big stones." Some claim that past-life regressions are structured through hypnotic suggestions by the hypnotherapist, but situations like the one above seem to happen as often as not when the hypnotherapist does inadvertently make a direct suggestion during a regression. Clients often do not pick up on suggestions like this. Just the same, suggesting anything that specific is probably a mistake that I and other past-life therapists try not to make (but sometimes do, anyway!).

Another reason I chose this transcript is that in it I ask Betty several questions that she does not directly answer. For example, regarding her home, I ask her:

T: . . . What's it made of?

B: It's attached to other homes.

T: All right. Like row houses?

B: I don't think it's the country.

Betty does not answer the questions I ask; she is analyzing the scene she is seeing in her own way, and apparently does not feel she must answer my questions as I ask them. The old idea that a hypnotized person can be led to say whatever the hypnotist wants is greatly exaggerated, and no past-life therapist (or any other hypnotherapist) believes it. Clients do things in their own ways, and they should.

The regression above turned out to be a life in France in the eighteenth century, but neither Betty nor I knew that when she first moved into it. All she knew was what she saw, and the past life continued to unfold in these visual, scene-by-scene ways.

I had instructed Betty's Upper Mind to let the magic chair land on an "average, ordinary day." For this reason (and probably this reason alone), Betty did not move into this past life in the midst of the traumatic event that was related to her therapy problem. Instead, she moved into the past life slowly and calmly at a neutral moment, and we were able to explore her home, her family, and her living situation in general before we even tried to access the traumatic event. By the time we did, she was able to place that event in its proper context in the life as a whole, and it was much less frightening than it would have been if we had plunged into it at the beginning, when neither of us would have had any idea of what was happening. I give the details of this and three of Betty's other past lives in Chapter 4.

In the following chapters, I discuss many past-life regressions, most of them explored for therapy. But people sometimes want to explore their past lives out of simple curiosity. It is sometimes thought that past lives can be explored only if there is some problem that needs healing, but that is not true. More and more people every year are simply curious about what past lives they have lived and what they may have learned in those other lives, and this curiosity is an excellent reason to explore your past lives. For these people, group workshops are probably best, as they are not only less expensive than private sessions but usually are not focused on problems that require individual therapy.

Be warned, however: Exploring your past lives for any reason, even for simple curiosity, is not like going to a movie that you will soon forget. Exploring any of your past lives will usually give you unexpected insights about some talent or interest or relationship, or perhaps some problem you hadn't really thought of in connection with past lives. I always warn people that exploring any of their past lives will change them whether they think so ahead of time or not. It will give them a new and wider view of life and of themselves, a deeper understanding from which there is no turning back.

CHAPTER FOUR

PHOBIAS

Do you have a phobia? How many people do you know who do? Phobias may be the most common form of psychological "problem" in the world: Untold millions suffer from them. If you have one, you know all too well what it is. But for those of you who don't, a phobia is an irrational fear of something that most other people do not fear: cats, perhaps, or water or caterpillars. The person with a phobia has little or no idea of what caused the phobia; if you ask, he or she will usually say, "Something in my childhood, I guess, but I don't remember, I've just always had it."

Phobias are sometimes confused with allergies. Allergies are physical reactions to something such as dust or pollen or a particular food, and although they can be very unpleasant, they are not phobias. I discuss past-life therapy for allergies and other physical problems in Chapter 9.

A phobia is different. A phobia is frightening in itself because it leads to panic attacks, and every phobia sufferer is afraid of those attacks themselves, as well as being afraid of the cat or the water. For those who don't know, here's how it works.

Take a man with a bad phobia for cats. He walks into a room with a cat in it, and the minute he sees it, he finds himself breathing faster and faster until he begins to hyperventilate, his hands shake and perspire, and his knees feel weak and about to collapse under him. He may feel dizzy or sick and may, in the worst (and very rare) case, actually pass out. He is terrified that he is about to have a heart attack or about to die, or lose control entirely and run howling and screaming from the room and make a complete fool of himself. This is called a panic attack, and it seems to happen all by itself, while everyone else in the room is petting and admiring the nice pretty kitty. Panic attacks just seem to take the phobic person over; people have no control over their own reactions, and nothing can be more terrifying than that.

So it doesn't help to have well-meaning friends tell the person to "just get over it, there's nothing to be afraid of, look how sweet the kitty is." People with phobias already know those things, rationally. They tell themselves those things more often than their friends tell them. But the phobia doesn't stop.

There are things we are all afraid of, like an out-of-control fire or a raging tiger charging at us. Fears like those are not really irrational. It is healthy to be afraid of those things; if we're afraid of them, we'll be careful to stay away from those situations. Fear is like pain: unpleasant, but it keeps us safer and living longer, because fear and pain lead us to avoid the causes of the fear and the pain.

But a phobia is an *irrational* fear. The man with the phobia for cats learns to avoid cats, *all* cats, *anywhere.* If he sees a cat walking down the street, he crosses to the other side; if you have a cat, he finds excuses not to visit you. By the time they are adults, most people with phobias have limited their activities, almost without realizing it. People with phobias for snakes or bugs will stay away from the woods and will never appreciate the beauty of nature; people with phobias for water will stay away from water and never learn to swim, never enjoy a boat ride or a simple day at the beach. And they do not even know what they are missing.

One of my clients, who had a phobia for caterpillars, hated summer because it was the caterpillar season. She never went outdoors in the summer without a large-brimmed hat (because caterpillars sometimes dropped from trees), made her husband and her three children brush themselves off before they came into the house, and watched every step she took because she might step on one of the hated things. She knew all this was limiting her life, she was ashamed of her own behavior, and she worried about how it might affect her children, but she still had no idea of the boundaries she had built around her life. After she got rid of the phobia, she discovered gardening, horseback riding, painting landscapes outdoors, and picnics and hiking with that same husband and children. Her life opened up when she no longer had the phobia, in ways she had not foreseen. She had been limiting herself more than she ever realized, as all phobia sufferers do.

Another bad thing about phobias is that people who have them are ashamed of them and try to hide them from others. They have learned that others often laugh at them, so they learn not to tell. Even when they come for therapy, they tell the therapist about the phobia as if they were confessing some wicked deed. They are afraid they are "crazy" or "weak-willed" because they cannot control their reactions, because they are afraid of this little, simple thing, a thing that other people think nothing of.

So far, I have mentioned only phobias for specific things, such as cats or caterpillars or water. But there are other kinds of phobias. There are three broad categories of phobias: specific phobias, social phobias, and agoraphobia. These are the categories listed in the current *Diagnostic and Statistical Manual* of the American Psychiatric Association. The three kinds are exactly what they sound like.

Specific phobias are fears of specific things, like the phobias for cats or water above. Social phobias, though, are fears of situations involving other people, like speaking in public. Some other fairly common social phobias are fears of eating in public, using public bathrooms, and being in a crowd. If they're severe enough, social phobias can limit a person's activities to nearly zero.

But perhaps the most limiting phobia of all is agoraphobia, the fear of leaving home. This often starts with panic attacks while the person is driving, although it may start in some other situation, and it gets worse until the person cannot leave his or her own home. Many people with agoraphobia have a "safe companion" they can leave home with, as long as the companion does the driving and never leaves them alone. But even with a safe companion, the person feels anxious while away from home. Such trips are no pleasure for them and they make them only if absolutely necessary. Some take antianxiety medications when they have to leave home, but many find that these either do not work well for them or create their own problems and they would rather not use them.

Agoraphobia is a seriously incapacitating condition. Sufferers cannot leave their homes to go to work, to shop, to visit others, to attend social functions, or to travel. And agoraphobia gets worse as the years roll by. Specific and social phobias tend not to get worse although they don't usually get better, either, without treatment. But agoraphobia gets worse if it's not healed, and the sufferer may eventually become self-imprisoned in a single room.

There are many treatments for all these kinds of phobias, some of them very effective. One of the most effective is proving to be past-life therapy, when the phobia has been caused by past-life experiences. But sometimes the source is in the person's present lifetime.

One man with a phobia for heights had learned to fear heights when he was very small because his older brothers had thought it was funny to swing him suspended by his feet over the stairwell. Nothing to do with past lives here. When he realized the source of the phobia, it pretty much disappeared, and he even forgave his brothers as being young and thoughtless at the time. A woman with a fear of the dark traced it back to her childhood years, when she would lie awake and frightened in her dark room listening to her parents' loud, angry fighting in the next room. This woman's phobia also disappeared. So not all phobias are caused by past life experiences.

But a good many are. In a study I carried out, 84 percent of the specific phobias and 60 percent of the social phobias were caused by past-life experiences, and after the people looked at those past-life experiences in hypnosis, their phobias pretty much disappeared. I mentioned above the woman with the phobia for caterpillars. Her fear was caused by past-life experiences. I describe them below. The woman is Betty, whose entry into one of her past lives I described in Chapter 3. The past-life events she found are typical of the kinds of events that cause specific phobias.

As I said in the previous chapter, I use a concept I call the client's "Upper Mind" as a guide in past-life work. Betty's Upper Mind said that she had lived twenty past lives in all, but that only four of them were responsible for her phobia for caterpillars. We examined those four, but not the other sixteen. I asked Betty's Upper Mind to choose the order in which they should be examined, and that order was not chronological. But I present them here in chronological order, with the order in which they were explored indicated in parentheses. It was the "Josh" life that Betty was entering in the excerpt given in Chapter 3. Chronologically, this was the earliest of the four phobia-related lives, but the last one that we examined.

Josh: 1731–1797, France (fourth examined). Josh grew up in a small town and became, like his father, a physician in the same town. One day he was called to treat a man who had badly injured his leg while chopping wood and had lain alone in the woods for two or three days. By the time he was found, the wound was infected and gangrenous and maggots had invaded it. Josh insisted that the man be brought back to the town, where Josh would find it easier to work. However, the trip was not an easy one, and by the time they arrived in the town, the man was almost dead. He did die later, after Josh had amputated the leg, and Josh blamed himself for insisting upon bringing the man back to the town instead of trying to treat him in the woods. He felt that the maggots had beaten him and he hated them. Josh was married and had four children, and he said that for the most part it was a happy life. He died at sixty-six, apparently of a heart attack.

Claire: 1821–1837, Great Britain (third examined). A happy young girl, Claire lived in a stable farming family. She died at sixteen when a teenaged boy was chasing her "in fun" with caterpillars in his hand, teasing her by threatening to put them on her back. Claire secretly liked the boy and hoped to marry him someday, but she slipped on wet grass and fell to her death down a clifflike ravine. After her death, as she hovered above her crumpled body at the foot of the ravine, she could see the boy sobbing and trying to shake her back to life.

Jenna: About 1845/1850–1890s, Europe (first examined). Jenna lived on a farm in what was possibly Austria. There were three incidents involving caterpillars in Jenna's life, all during a summer of bad caterpillar infestation when Jenna was ten years old. The three incidents were (1) seeing caterpillars everywhere outside; (2) seeing other children catching and crushing caterpillars in their fingers, which disgusted Jenna; and (3) going outdoors one day and getting caterpillars in her hair. When she tried to brush them out, they made a mess in her hair. This third incident was especially important, because her mother scolded her for her "stupidity" instead of comforting her and helping her to clean her hair. Jenna felt this was unfair of her mother, who had asked her to go outdoors to do some chore even though Jenna had not wanted to go out because of the caterpillars. Jenna grew up and became a farm wife, and came to terms with caterpillars. However, she said they were never as bad again as they had been during that one year. In that life Jenna hated caterpillars but she did not fear them; she said that she had "no choice" because caterpillars were there and there was nothing she could do about them. Jenna died in her bed in her forties, of an unspecified illness.

John: 1902–1937, Eastern United States, a railroad town (second examined). In his very early years, John was raised by both parents in a pleasant apartment, but his mother either died in childbirth or ran away when John was very young; exactly which is not clear. John said his father would not speak of it. In any case, when John was about twelve, he and his father moved to a shack by the railroad tracks, and his father did odd jobs for the railroad. John did the same work starting in his teens, loading and unloading freight cars and doing any other work he could find. The caterpillar incident had occurred in his teen years, when he and some other boys were burning caterpillar tents in a farmer's orchard. (This was a common way of getting rid of caterpillars in those days. A torch was made of rags, kerosene, and a long pole, lighted, and held up into the tree branches, to burn the caterpillar tents.) Some flaming bits had fallen onto John's back, burning him severely before the other boys could slap the fire out. Since the boys were not supposed to be burning the tents, John was afraid to tell anyone about his injury, and could get no treatment for it. Eventually it healed, but not without much pain and probably infection. John lived to the age of thirty-five, when he died in a fight with another man along the railroad tracks. He never married and never moved from the shack he and his father had shared.

An interesting thing about Betty's regression as John is that Betty has a birthmark on her back in the same place that the burning tent fell. I knew that Dr. Ian Stevenson had found birthmarks sometimes connected to children's memories of violent injuries in past lives, so this interested me. Betty at first said that she had a birthmark on her back but that it was on the wrong side. However, when we looked, it turned out that she had remembered the birthmark wrongly. After all, it was on her back, and she had never really seen it except in mirrors. But it was on the same side and in the same place where the burning tent had fallen on John's back.

What can we deduce from these four past lives? For one thing, there is the centuries-long development of a phobia. Josh, the eighteenth-century small-town doctor, developed a hatred rather than a fear of maggots. Maggots are not really caterpillars (at least, they do not turn into butterflies or moths, but flies). But they are similar in appearance to some small caterpillars. In her regression, Betty likened them to the small pale caterpillars that she had sometimes found on fresh vegetables, to her intense disgust. In the chronologically second of the four past lives, Betty's life as Claire, caterpillars were associated with her death in that life. The boy was carrying them in his hand as he chased her, teasing, and as she fell to her death down the ravine. Betty did not think Claire had really been afraid of them, although she disliked them; rather, the two young people were playing a flirtatious game, and Claire was only pretending to be afraid for the sake of the game. Nevertheless, because they were associated with her death in that lifetime, Betty began to have a little fear of them.

In the third of the four past lives, Jenna experienced a year of heavy caterpillar infestation. She had reactions to the caterpillars that were different from those of the other children. The other children played with them, albeit cruelly, and did not mind them. Jenna, on the other hand, found them repugnant, disgusting, and frightening, and this may indicate that a phobia had developed even then, caused by her experiences in the earlier Josh and Claire lives. Then in the Jenna life she had an especially unpleasant experience with them when she tried to brush them out of her hair. However, Jenna's real emotional reaction centered more on her mother's impatient scolding than on the caterpillars in her hair themselves. Jenna wanted comfort and help in cleaning her hair, but her mother treated her roughly and scolded her for getting them in her hair.

It is possible, although we will never know, that if Jenna's mother had been more helpful and sympathetic, the phobia might have been forestalled from ever developing further, even given John's experience in Betty's most recent life. Another thing about the Jenna life is that the other children laughed at Jenna for her dislike of their "games" with the caterpillars, calling her humiliating names. This is something that we should all realize: The ways in which we treat children's reactions and fears can help to shape a developing phobia (or other problem) for centuries to come, or possibly nip it in the bud.

In the John life, Betty's most recent life before she was born as Betty, we see again an unpleasant experience with caterpillars, the burn on John's back. John hated caterpillars and was afraid of them before that happened, and the burn experience deepened both the fear and the hatred. After the burn, John tried to avoid caterpillars. He never took part in tent burning again, and he became very alert to them. John died in 1937, and Betty herself was born in 1948, after an eleven-year "turnaround," or intermission, time.

What we see in these four past lives is behaviorism in action. According to the theories of behaviorism, people learn things, both good and bad, because of "reinforcements," repeated experiences that either reinforce or discourage ideas and actions. In the case of these four past lives, each lifetime's unpleasant experience added its bit to Betty's feelings about caterpillars: Her hatred and then her fear were reinforced by each of those experiences in its turn.

OTHER THERAPIES FOR PHOBIAS

As I said above, there are various treatments for specific phobias, other than past-life therapy, and some of them are very effective. One of the best is exposure therapy (sometimes called successive approximation therapy), in which the person is gradually exposed to the feared object or situation, and learns to control the anxiety in slow stages. Our man above with the phobia for cats, for example, will first look at pictures of cats and be taught to breathe deeply and calmly as he does so; then he will go into a room with a kitten in a cage at the other end of the room, breathing deeply and calmly all the while; then he will gradually get closer to the kitten, and finally he will graduate to a full-grown cat out of the cage. This method takes several sessions and a certain amount of homework, practicing the breathing techniques and looking at cats from safe distances, but eventually the man will be able to at least tolerate cats in the same room, as long as he remembers to breathe the way he has been taught. If he persists, he may actually begin to like cats, at least a little. But even if that doesn't happen (and it usually doesn't), he will be able to control his anxiety attacks, and that's important.

Another useful therapy for phobias is called systematic desensitization. This treatment was developed by Joseph Wolpe in the 1950s and is based upon his idea that a person cannot remain tense and fearful while in a physically relaxed state. It can be very helpful, especially in cases where it is not possible to schedule repeated direct exposure to the feared object or situation. Fears of flying or of lightning storms, for example, are often treated by systematic desensitization.

In systematic desensitization the client is taught a method of deep relaxation and in that state he or she experiences the same process of gradual approach described above for exposure therapy, but instead of experiencing the feared object or event in reality, he or she imagines them while in the relaxed state. After a while the idea of flying or lightning storms will no longer be frightening. Systematic desensitization has a long and fairly successful history, but for situations where direct exposure therapy is possible, research shows that it is usually more effective.

Both exposure therapy and systematic desensitization developed from behaviorism, and they both have had some success. Past-life therapy, however, has developed on its own, and seems to have even greater success.

Behaviorists have long believed that phobias develop from several unpleasant experiences with the feared object or situation, but they have not considered past-life experience as part of that process. But for many people with phobias, examining their past experiences in this present life yields few events that could have caused the phobia. At this point, it is said that "if we only knew *all* the things that really happened to this person, we would know the causes of the phobia." However, the behaviorists also acknowledge that we never can really know all that has happened to a person. So obviously, for a behaviorist, it is impossible to ever know the true causes of a phobia.

What's more, a behaviorist will tell you it doesn't matter if either the person or the therapist knows what caused it; even without knowing the cause, a phobia can often be treated or at least re-duced to a manageable level by direct exposure therapy or system-atic desensitization.

But past-life therapy for phobias shows us another picture. It seems that the behaviorists are both right and wrong. They're right that the phobia was caused by several unpleasant experiences with the feared object or situation, only the experiences happened dur-ing various past lives, not all in the present one. But they're wrong that it doesn't matter if the person or the therapist knows what caused the phobia. It may not really matter if the therapist knows; I think the real healing is done by the person and his or her Upper Mind, and the therapist is just a guide. But in regression work, the whole point is that the person must find all those unpleasant expe-riences that happened in their past lives. So the behaviorists are wrong on this point, in my opinion. It does matter that the person with the phobia find the true, past-life causes of the phobia. Once those are known, the phobia dissolves.

"Dissolve" is a good way to describe what happens. For example, in Betty's case, we examined the four relevant past lives during four separate sessions, and in the summer, too, when caterpillars were nibbling at our trees. As she came in for each session, she would tell me about something that had happened during the previous week that indicated that the phobia was "dissolving." Before her fourth and last session, she said that she didn't think she needed the session at all, because she had seen some caterpillars on a tree and barely noticed them until she had walked past them. She had come in only because her Upper Mind had said there were four past lives that had caused the phobia, and she was curious about what the fourth past life would be like. It turned out to be the Josh life, the one involving maggots.

I called Betty about five years later, to see how she was doing. We had an interesting exchange. We talked a bit about her family and general matters; then I asked, "How are you getting along with caterpillars these days?"

There was a long pause. Then she laughed.

"Do you know?" she said. "I'd forgotten that I was ever afraid of caterpillars!"

Betty's phobia had "dissolved," and this is not a result that is usually attained with either exposure therapy or systematic desensitization.

Betty told me that her life had opened up for her since our work. She is the one I mentioned earlier who now gardens, rides horseback, paints outdoors, hikes, picnics, and generally enjoys her life indoors and out, in summer as well as winter. And caterpillars no longer bother her.

So the behaviorists are right when they say that phobias are built from several unpleasant experiences, and each experience teaches the person once again the lesson that "that thing is dangerous, bad, scary, and I hate it and fear it." But the experiences may stretch back centuries and occur in past lives, not this one. I think it takes more than one unpleasant experience to build a specific phobia; in my own research study of people with phobias, the average number of unpleasant experiences in past lives the people reported was between three and four.

This makes sense. After all, if phobias developed from only one unpleasant experience, we should all be afraid of everything, because we have all had many unpleasant experiences in our present lives. Yet we're not afraid of everything. It takes several unpleasant experiences, and usually over two or more past lives, and as each one builds on the ones before, the lesson to "fear this" gets stronger and stronger and we take it with us like unconscious baggage from life to life.

It probably also takes a trigger to set it off. By "trigger" I do not mean the causes of the phobia; I mean the incident that sets the phobia off in the present life, as a trigger sets off a loaded gun just waiting to be fired. In Betty's case, we never found the trigger and didn't even look for it, for it doesn't really seem to be necessary to find it. But I think there always is a trigger, whether we look for it or not. We can only guess, but for Betty it was most likely her first sight of a caterpillar, or even a picture of one, that acted as the trigger. It is usually something like that, something that was seemingly unimportant at the time it happened and is not even consciously remembered. It became important only because it acted as the trigger that set the phobia off.

However, I have worked with innumerable people with phobias who, like Betty, have freed themselves from their fears by exploring the past-life connections but with whom we never looked for a trigger at all. What is necessary is that the person find out the past-life causes. Simply becoming aware of those causes seems to be enough.

Social phobias more often seem to have causes in the early years of the present life than specific phobias do. In my study of phobias, 84 percent of the specific phobias had past-life causes, while only 60 percent of the social phobias did. But the kinds of incidents that caused the social phobias are very similar, whether the events occurred in this life or a past one. They are different from the kinds of incidents that caused the specific phobias, too. The specific phobias were caused by one-time events in the past lives, such as Claire's fall down the ravine, or the burning tents falling on John's back. The social phobias were usually caused by ongoing social conditions in either the present or the past life.

For example, one woman with a fear of eating in restaurants traced her fear to her childhood in her present life, when her family ate frequently in restaurants and she felt that people always stared at them as they threaded their way through the crowded rooms. She was also always afraid she would make some mistake in table manners since her parents would publicly scold her for this. Another woman traced her fear of speaking in groups to a past life in which she was a hardworking and lonely pioneer woman. She was the butt of jokes and had been laughed at by her father, brother, and later, her husband whenever she spoke up (and therefore, she never did speak up). Both of these causes for social phobias were ongoing conditions in these people's lives, whether past or present. They happened over and over in both cases, and the person could do nothing about them. For both of these women, becoming aware of the causes of their social phobias relieved their fears.

Agoraphobia seems to have a different cause entirely. For years I had found that although specific and social phobias often had past-life causes and disappeared after those causes were explored in hypnosis, agoraphobia was not always related to a past life, nor could we always find a present life cause either. But sometimes this serious phobia *was* related to a past life.

For example, one woman I worked with had agoraphobia and a fear of strangers as well, a social phobia. She reported two past lives, both as women, in which she had left her home alone and had unpleasant experiences with strangers. In one life, strangers had knocked her down and stolen her purse, and in the other, strangers had attempted to rape her (but not succeeded). Even though neither of these experiences resulted in her death or in any physical injury except for slight bruises, they were both terrifying to this woman's past-life selves and the lesson she had learned from both of these past-life experiences was that if you leave your home alone, strangers can hurt you. After exploring these two past lives, she left those ideas in the past. So sometimes agoraphobia is connected to a past life, and when it is, exploring that life (or lives) can dissolve the agoraphobia.

But in many cases, I had found that agoraphobia did not seem to be caused by past-life experiences, or by experiences earlier in the client's present life either. Sometimes clients went back in hypnosis to some childhood event that they consciously thought might have caused the agoraphobia, but doing that did not get rid of their fear. So I suspected that the childhood event we had explored had not been the true cause.

Then in 1992, *The Journal of Regression Therapy* published a case study of an agoraphobic client by a past-life therapist in the Netherlands, Dr. Marianne de Jong. De Jong's client had reported a very unusual cause for her fear, after which her agoraphobia had disappeared. I tested this in my study of phobias, and sure enough, 63 percent of the agoraphobics turned out to report the same cause de Jong had found, and after they did, their agoraphobia disappeared, just as had happened with de Jong's client. This cause is intriguing and very different from the causes for any other condition that I know of. De Jong calls it the "lost soul interlife" scenario.

These agoraphobics report that after one of their past lives (usually their most recent one), they did not know that they had died. What's more, they never did find it out. Instead they floated aimlessly for a time after their death in the past life and then found themselves drawn into a small body (a fetus, as it always turned out). Thus they were born into this present lifetime still caught in the last one, never realizing that they had finished the previous life and begun a new one, the present life.

They are not happy with this aimless floating experience. Confused and sometimes frightened, they believe they are still alive and cannot understand what is happening to them. They may see people but not be able to make contact with them, or they may see no one, instead feeling themselves utterly alone in a timeless and formless space with no boundaries and no safe and solid place to rest. Truly a strange and frightening experience.

One interesting thing about this experience is that after we finally reach the past life the person has left, it turns out that he or she died either very suddenly or while unconscious.

I will give a couple of examples of this experience. When his magic chair stopped, one agoraphobic man found himself floating high above a mountainous scene of forest and cliffs and a path, all of which he could clearly see below. But try as he might, he could not get back down to the ground, and he felt confused and afraid. Eventually he drifted off into gray fog. When I directed him to "go ahead to the next important thing that happens," he found himself in the tiny body of a fetus and felt secure again to be within boundaries. But he was unaware that he had finished one life and begun another.

When we finally got to the truth of the matter, it developed that in his most recent life, as a farmer in New Zealand, he had been walking on a path on top of a cliff when he was struck by lightning. To him, one minute he had been walking on the path, the next minute he was floating high above the scene. He had no idea what had happened, no memory of the lightning strike, and had never realized that he had died in that lifetime.

A woman, when we first went back to "the moment when the floating began," saw an "old woman sleeping in a bed." When I directed her to go ahead to the "next important thing that happens," she found herself in the tiny body of a fetus, and felt secure there, but had no realization that she was starting a new life. Directing her to move back again to where the "sleeping" woman was, I asked her to look closely at the woman, and more closely, until at last she said, "You know, I think she's dead." When I asked, "Who is that woman?" my client considered this for a minute or two and then announced, "I think she's me."

We were ready now to explore that past life, and after we had done so, I directed the client to move quickly through the death experience. It turned out that the past-life woman had been extremely ill and in a coma, and she had been floating in and out of her body for some time before she died. Finally, she had just stayed out and had never realized what had happened.

What seems to be important for agoraphobics is for them to finally recognize that the past life is over and that a new life, usually the present life, has begun.

As I said, this lost-soul scenario seems to be unique to agoraphobics. For other phobias, and for some agoraphobics as well, events in one or more past lives seem to have caused the problem, and examining those events usually makes the problem dissolve. But for many agoraphobics, the lost-soul scenario seems to be the cause, and examining it dissolves the agoraphobia. I have worked with many agoraphobics who have related this scenario, and who have called me within a day or two to report that their agoraphobia was gone.

But sometimes a bit of "supportive therapy" in the form of some new learning is needed, too. This is not true for some problems, such as many specific phobias; after all, living without a fear of caterpillars or cats does not take any new skills (although it does widen one's world).

But some problems do need some additional help, some practice at doing the thing that was feared for so long. Put simply, the woman who is finally free of a lifelong fear of water had better not jump off the diving board before she learns to swim! In the same way, a fear of public speaking may disappear after the past-life (or present-life) causes are examined, but the person still does not know how to make an effective speech, even though he or she no longer fears the experience. Swimming and effective public speaking require skills that must be learned, and the person has to learn them if he or she is to stay afloat in either situation. In the case of agoraphobics, many have kept their driving licenses up-to-date for purposes of identification, but those who haven't must go through the usual driving program and get a new license. And if they have been agoraphobic for a long time, a few quick refresher lessons in driving might be a good idea, too!

Dr. Rick Levy, while a member of the Board of Directors of the Association for Past Life Research and Therapies, commented that "the trouble with past-life therapy is that no one believes it." He's right. But when it works, and it often does, it works fast and thoroughly.

Just why it works so well is not really known. But it seems almost automatic. The person does not need to learn any special relaxation breathing techniques to face the future and doesn't need to do any homework to eliminate the fear. And once it's gone, it's gone. After twenty years, I have been able to check up on clients from many years ago, and their phobias have not returned. As Betty said on the phone five years after our work, "Do you know, I'd forgotten that I was ever afraid of caterpillars."

There are still other ways in which people with phobias are sometimes treated. Some forms of therapy have considered phobias as being symbolic of a fear of something else. A fear of snakes, for example, has traditionally been believed to reflect a fear of sexual activity if you are a woman, and a fear of your own sexual impulses if you are a man. Past-life therapy does not support this idea. When I have dealt with phobias for snakes, the causes have almost always been bad experiences with real snakes in past lives.

The only exceptions are what I might call cases of mistaken identity: when the past-life person thinks a snake is involved but is wrong about this. As an example, I think of a man with a phobia for snakes who in his most recent past life touched a wet rope in a dark cellar and panicked, believing it to be a snake when it rolled under his hand. He was already a bit phobic for snakes, from experiences in two earlier past lives, and this rope experience in his most recent past life had contributed the final touch to his already developing phobia.

The only connection between sexuality and snakes I have ever heard in past-life work is a little past-life girl who was sexually abused by a man who warned her "not to tell" or he would let "the snake" out to bite her. He kept this "snake" in his trousers, of course, and the young child had really believed the snake was a real one. Mistaken identity again, but this past-life experience had contributed to that client's fear of snakes.

Phobia treatments that are based upon the idea above, that phobias are reflections of fears of something else, something hidden, take many sessions of insight therapy to work through the various possibilities. And in the end, these treatments have not turned out to be very effective. You can learn much about yourself in such a form of therapy, and it can be rewarding in many ways, but it does little to eliminate phobias. So if that is your primary goal and your time and money are limited, you might try either exposure therapy, systematic desensitization, or past-life therapy first.

In the next chapter I discuss another set of disorders that often turn out to stem from past-life experiences: eating disorders.

CHAPTER FIVE

EATING DISORDERS

There are many types of eating disorders, and they are very different from each other. In this chapter I discuss obesity, anorexia nervosa, bulimia, and innate cravings or aversions for particular foods. Considering that we must eat to live, we seem to have a lot of trouble doing so wisely. We seem to bring some of this trouble with us from our past lives, but not all of it. I will say first that with the more serious eating problems, such as anorexia and bulimia, most past-life therapists, like myself, require that the person be under a physician's care before they will work with him or her.

I will discuss obesity first. Obesity is usually defined as a state of being more than 20 percent to 30 percent over one's recommended weight, but a good many people in our culture are just plain overweight without reaching the levels that would be called obese by that definition. Suggested causes for obesity (or just being fat) have ranged from the psychological to the physical.

An old idea, and still popular, comes from psychoanalysis. It is that the obese person, at an unconscious level of the mind, desires to be fat (and therefore, supposedly, sexually unattractive) to avoid sexual involvement. A similar idea is that the person is trying to avoid all adult social responsibilities, sexual or otherwise. Other ideas are that the person unconsciously hates him- or herself or feels insecure and that overeating is an attempt to find comfort while at the same time protecting the fragile self from assault. I think of these theories as "fat as armor" theories. And of course, there have always been what can be called the "moral shiftlessness" explanations: The person lacks that much-admired virtue, self-control, or is too lazy to prepare proper meals or to get enough exercise.

Physically, most recently we hear the idea that some gland or hormone is not functioning properly and prevents the person from ever feeling full, so he eats too much too often. It is also believed that obesity may sometimes have a genetic basis; that it runs in families.

There is a strong cultural element in overeating. Food is a lot more important to us than we usually realize, and it always has been. If you think of our long human history, you see that eating and food have been much more than mere necessities for survival. All cultures everywhere have used food as part of social interactions and ceremony, and we still do.

Overeating is a complicated problem that may be caused by complex combinations of elements, and it is reinforced by the very society we live in today. It seems that we don't need any more possible explanations for it; we have plenty already. But there is another possible explanation: that a past-life experience may sometimes cause it.

Jane was a client who needed to lose about fifty pounds to reach her recommended weight. She was clinically obese and had been overweight all her life. Over the years she had tried "every diet known to man" and had lost some weight for short periods of time with some of the diets, but sooner or later she slipped off the diet and put the weight back on again. She knew she ate uncontrollably when she felt criticized or even mildly questioned at work, and snacked to comfort herself during the evenings at home. But lately it seemed that she was always eating—snacking in the car and stopping at drive-in junk food places on and off throughout the day as she drove around on her job.

Jane would eat anything, but had special cravings for salty things and sweets. Because of her weight and her many failures in her attempts to control her overeating, she felt depressed, hopeless, and at the mercy of her constant compulsion to eat. In hypnosis, her Upper Mind said she had one past life related to her overeating. We went back to the following sad story.

Jane reported a life in the 1800s as "Sally." Sally was born in Ohio in 1832, and her early years were spent happily in the comfortable farmhouse and the green fields of the family farm. But Sally had been born with a deformed leg and had trouble walking. From her early years she realized that her brother, John, four or five years older than she, was her father's favorite child and that she was considered useless. She was close to her mother, who gave her the love and attention she needed, but her father was distant and preoccupied with his own affairs.

When Sally was six, her father "lost his money," in what way Sally did not know. He decided to move his family west, as so many did, looking for what they thought would be the magic land. They settled in Oklahoma, on a homestead that was dry in summer and cold in winter and hopeless for farming at any time. Sally's father, like many other Western settlers of the time, had bought the land sight unseen, and although he tried, with the help of her brother, to make a success of it, he ended up failing, both because the land was so poor and because he knew little about farming under those conditions. He apparently became increasingly desperate and took his anger and frustration out on the "useless" Sally and to some extent on his wife, becoming violent and abusive toward both of them.

When Jane entered this past life, it was as the ten-year-old Sally, living in the rough cabin the family had built in Oklahoma. It was a life of extreme privation. Asked to go to a mealtime, Sally described a bleak meal with "no one talking." They were eating a kind of "thin porridge" that was "very bland." Later, Jane said it had no salt because they had none.

Asked about food issues in general, Sally said:

Sally: There was never enough—we were very poor—they always gave everything to my brother—

Therapist: They gave everything to your brother?

S: Uh-huh—

T: And you just got whatever was left over?

S: Yeah, right.

T: Was there anything you could do about it? Could you get food anywhere else?

S: No—I got berries.

T: You got berries. But—were you hungry a lot of the time?

S: I was always hungry. I used to steal food.

T: You used to steal food—where did you steal it from?

S: The kitchen.

T: The kitchen. And you'd get away with it?

S: No, no, I'd get beaten.

T: You'd get beaten. How'd your mother feel about that?

S: She couldn't do anything.

T: Did she ever sneak you anything?

S: Sometimes.

T: Okay. What kinds of things did she sneak you?

S: Cake, sometimes a cookie, bread.

I thought that Sally's reference to cake and cookies was inconsistent with her description of their extreme poverty, but when I asked Jane, after the regression, what they were like, she described them as flat cakes made of flour and water and baked in a frying pan, something like pancakes. If they filled the whole pan, they were "cakes"; if they were smaller, they were "cookies."

Sally died at ten. Her father hurled a "big pot" at her when she asked for salt; of course, they had none. She fell and hit her head on the table edge and died instantly.

Asked to describe herself, Jane described Sally as "skinny; she had freckles." Then she said:

S: She had something wrong with her leg.

T: She had something wrong with her leg? Become aware of that.

S: She couldn't walk right.

T: Couldn't walk right. Was that something she was born with or something that happened to her?

S: Something she was born with, she walked with a limp.

T: And how'd she feel about that?

S: She hated it.

One interesting thing about this regression was that Jane, as Sally, spoke sometimes in the first person, as "I," and at other times in the third person, as "she." You can see this in the transcript excerpts above. This shift into the third person was not in response to any direction from me to "see things objectively," a direction I sometimes give but did not in this case. Jane was distancing herself from the more unpleasant parts of the memory, something clients often do.

Later, when I asked Sally what she most wanted, she said she wanted to be a dancer. She had seen dancing back in Ohio, and had wished she could move with the same grace and beauty. She said:

S: I like pretty things. I like flowers—I like dancing. I like things to look pretty.

T: There was very little of that in your life, wasn't there.

S: It was very ugly.

When I asked Jane what lessons she had taken out of that lifetime, she said she had learned "not to ask for things." But she also said she had learned "to be sure of myself." When asked what lessons she had learned about food, she said, "I want it all," meaning her brother's share as well as hers, meaning everything in sight.

This past-life regression defused many of Jane's compulsive eating habits, after which she began to eat more sensibly and lose weight. She saw the connections between Sally's father's criticisms and her own reactions to criticism, between Sally's feelings of hopelessness and her own, between Sally's constant hunger and her own feelings of never being full. The message "I want it all" is considerably weakened, and gets more so as time passes. Jane also dares to "ask for things" more than she did, and she is working on overcoming that message entirely. Those old feelings have become part of the past, not the present. And she likes the other lesson, "to be sure of myself"; it gives her strength, as well it might.

Jane has done well, losing her excess weight slowly and steadily. She comes to see me every few months for reinforcement, for which I use more conventional techniques, and for a little basic support, something we all need from time to time. But now she feels more in control of her own eating habits, and recognizes the old ways for what they were: sad little Sally's ways, and not her own.

Jane's case is a good example of a situation where the past-life regression explained her problem and loosened its grip on her, but where she needed a little continuing supportive therapy afterward to help her meet her goal. And Jane continues to work to overcome the negative messages she carried forward from Sally's short and tragic life.

Not all obese people find past-life connections with their eating habits. But those who were "fat kids" usually do, especially if they were fat kids in a thin family. And many people who have been "roller-coasters" (as they often say) all their lives find past-life connections, too. The past lives are usually similar to Jane's: a situation in which the person was deprived of food for a long period of time, as Sally was. I have never known an obese person to go back to a past-life situation in which the food deprivation was short-term, such as starvation, although one might think such an experience could create an overeating compulsion. Famine or starvation in past lives does not usually seem to be related to overeating and obesity. It is, however, sometimes related to another eating disorder, anorexia nervosa.

Anorexia nervosa, often called simply anorexia, is probably the most serious eating disorder there is. It is life-threatening and, sadly, often fatal. It usually begins in the person's adolescence. Although it is popularly believed to be a young girl's disease, young boys fall prey to it, too. The youngster simply stops eating, or eats so little that normal body weight cannot be sustained, let alone the growth that should occur during adolescence. What eating is done may become ritualized, with tiny portions measured out and carefully arranged on special plates at certain times.

Bulimia, the practice of self-induced vomiting after eating, sometimes accompanies anorexia, and any anorectic who seems to be eating properly needs to be watched carefully after meals to prevent her sneaking off to the bathroom and getting rid of the food she ate by inducing vomiting. Another common way of getting rid of the food is by taking large doses of laxatives. Eventually, if anorexia is untreated (and sometimes even if it is treated), the person can gradually come near to starving to death, or succumb to opportunistic diseases as the whole system weakens. Anorexia is such a serious disease that parents should be alert to any teenager who suddenly begins to lose weight too fast or cuts his or her food intake severely. It is a disease that needs to be nipped in the bud, and it won't go away all by itself. Anorectics should be under a doctor's care from the moment a parent suspects the condition.

Like obesity, there have been many explanations for anorexia in young women. The major explanations are of two kinds, one centering on the family and the general environment, the other a more psychological explanation. In a family or a culture in which being thin is seen as a desirable goal for a woman, young girls may fight the natural development of their bodies during adolescence by refusing to eat properly, and thus stay thin. Our society encourages the ideal of the overly thin woman, of course, and when a girl's family and her friends encourage it too, she faces a lot of pressure to be thin. This may be more common for girls, but boys experience their own version of this problem. For instance, boys are often encouraged to be "fit," and this is often equated with being thin. A more psychological explanation is that these youngsters, boys or girls, unconsciously want to stay children and are fighting the natural growth and sexual development of their bodies. It works: With this disease, their bodies do not develop sexually as they should. Sex is scary for most teenagers, and remaining physically a child may seem like a safe way to avoid it.

There have been various physiological explanations, too, such as faulty appetite regulation mechanisms, but it is often difficult for researchers to see these clearly because by the time many anorectic girls or boys are under medical treatment, damage has already been done to the regulatory systems. Thus, it is hard to know which came first, the damage or the anorexia.

There have been different past-life experiences reported as being related to anorexia. One past-life therapist, Dr. Alfred

Hoffmann, reported a case in which an anorectic girl of sixteen had experienced two past lives that may have caused the anorexia. In the first, in the 1700s, she had died of what was probably stomach cancer (unrecognized as such at the time) and the feeling of heaviness and "being stuffed" was associated with great pain and distention of her stomach. In the second, in the 1800s, she had died of painful food poisoning following a picnic. Examining these two past lives, coupled with Dr. Hoffmann's direct hypnotic suggestion that she "give back to that body what belonged to it and leave it there," did the trick and the girl recovered from her anorexia.

This client also suffered from an aversion to eggs and egg salads, and she was sometimes bulimic. Dr. Hoffmann notes that the food that gave the past-life person food poisoning at the picnic in the past life was egg salad. But there had also been a triggering experience in the client's early teen years. In hypnosis, she remembered that her anorexia had begun abruptly at the wake for an aunt, when she was fourteen. She had seen the body, which had a distended abdomen, and at the same time heard people in the next room laughing and talking and eating. Although Dr. Hoffmann does not say this, I wonder if there was the smell of food in the air as well. In any case, this was the triggering incident. The young girl's stomach began to ache and she vomited, and for the next two years, until she recalled the two past lives above, she was anorectic, and sometimes bulimic.

There are not as many adult anorectics but there are a few, and a client of mine, Helen, was such a one. Helen had suffered from anorexia since her teens, and had been in and out of various forms of treatment for years. When I worked with her, she was in her thirties and had learned to eat just barely enough to stay alive. She did not suffer from bulimia, and never had. Her meals, such as they were, were highly ritualized, measured out, and eaten carefully. Eating was a religious experience for her, and with each bite she recited a special prayer to God. She lived an isolated life, with little contact with others. After a few frightening experiences of hospitalization, she knew her physical systems were beginning to break down and decided it was time for her to be free of the anorexia. She came to me to see if exploring any of her past lives could help.

Helen went back into a past life in which she had been a nun during a war somewhere in Europe in the 1700s. The nuns were sheltering refugees from the general chaos, and as their food had begun to run low, the nuns had begun to sacrifice their own allotment of food for the others. Although the other nuns did not go entirely without food, she herself came to believe that God wanted this sacrifice from her, and she made it, finally dying of starvation, and feeling at peace, a martyr.

This past life explained not only the anorexia but also the religious significance Helen placed upon her eating habits. Religious mysticism is not uncommon among anorectics, and there may be many such past lives waiting to be found.

Beth, another client, had more recent past-life connections to her anorexia. Beth was in her late teens and had suffered from anorexia for three or four years. Like Helen, she was not bulimic. Also like Helen, she reported a past life in which she had sacrificed herself for others, in this case, for her two children. Beth reported a past life as a Holocaust victim, a mother in a concentration camp who had given whatever food she could get to her children. She never learned if the children had survived the camp.

Another client, a young man named Phil, came for another problem but I suspected that he was possibly anorectic, although I did not tell him that. Much too thin, he spent hours every day working out and running, and he was a strict vegetarian who planned his meals carefully.

He went back to a past life in which he had become the leader of a small Native American group after the older leader died. They were trying to reach safety over snowy mountains in the winter, and somehow he had led them the wrong way and they were lost, although he did not tell the others so. They had little food, and he, as leader, had felt responsible for their condition. He had eaten wild grass and left what food they had for the others. Finally, he had collapsed and died from hunger, cold, and exhaustion, feeling that he had let his people down because he was not strong enough to go on.

The problem Phil had come to me for involved his feeling that he had to be responsible for everything and do everything exactly right, and this past life was certainly relevant to that, but it was also relevant to his present need to stay fit and strong and to his possible anorexia. Phil and I never did mention anorexia, but when he called a few weeks later, he said he felt much more relaxed and as if the burden of being responsible for everything and everybody was gone. He also volunteered that he no longer felt he had to exercise quite so much to stay fit, or stick to a vegetarian diet quite so strictly. I have often wondered if Phil has gotten fat since then; I hope not!

Helen, Beth, and Phil all starved to death in their past lives, and in all three cases it was done willingly and knowingly, as a sacrifice for others. I have worked with many other clients who have starved to death in a past life, but who have not been anorectic in this life. The factor of starving may not be enough in itself, but must perhaps be coupled with the "willing sacrifice," or with some feeling of personal responsibility for others, something all three of these clients shared in their past lives. In all of these cases, the past-life characters had deliberately sacrificed themselves for others. For Helen, as the nun she felt that God required her sacrifice; in Beth's case, she was a mother trying to save her children; and Phil had felt responsible for the group's situation so he ate grass rather than food so the others would have what food there was.

In Dr. Hoffmann's case, however, we see a different picture. His client's two past-life characters had died painfully, in one case from stomach cancer, in the other from food poisoning. But neither had made a sacrifice for others. On the other hand, Dr. Hoffmann's client had a known aversion to a certain type of food, eggs and egg salad, and she was also bulimic, problems that Helen, Beth, and Phil did not share.

There is not much anecdotal evidence about anorexia and past lives, and not too many anorectics present themselves for past-life therapy. Nor has any research on them been done to assess how many cases are caused by past-life experiences. So it is hard to fine-tune what kinds of past lives they might go back to. But in the cases above, we may see some of the possible past-life causes of this tragic disease.

Whatever the truth, three of these clients, Dr. Hoffmann's client and Helen and Beth, have begun to eat again, and have stopped their obsessive behavior about food. And Phil seemed to have lost his obsessive focusing on being fit and eating sparingly. Dr. Hoffmann's client, whom he saw in 1984, is healthy, married, and has three children; Beth is likewise married and has one child, and

Helen, although still living a somewhat isolated life, is eating normally and is involved with her artwork.

In all of these cases, the more conventional explanations I gave above seem not to be particularly relevant to the anorexia. It may be that they were all born into families that stressed the importance of thinness for women or fitness for men, and our society certainly reinforces both of those ideas. Or it may be that they all had a fear of developing sexually. However, being thin or fear of sex were not issues in any of their past-life reports, and two of the three women have since married and had children. Phil did not mention any sexual problems, although he may have had some. So I question the relevance of those conventional explanations to some cases of anorexia.

Bulimia is, as I have said, a part of some cases of anorexia nervosa, but not of all. As it was with Dr. Hoffmann's client, bulimia may sometimes be the first sign of anorexia. Bulimia is said to be fashionable among adolescent girls today, many of whom are all too conscious of their weight, and I have heard college girls say that "everybody in the dorm does it." In a determined young girl, it may sometimes mark the beginning of the serious problem of anorexia. A less-determined young girl may well try it once or twice and decide it's not for her. After all, vomiting is not pleasant, nor is severe purging with laxatives.

There is another pattern that can occur with bulimia, the gorge-and-purge pattern. This form of bulimia is found among adult women as well as teenagers, but seems rare in boys or men. It may be what some of the college girls I mentioned above do. People with this behavior pattern do not fear food or dislike it. Their problem is just the opposite: they love certain foods and gorge on them. Then they feel stuffed and to relieve the discomfort they purge themselves. Although this behavior is not good for the body and can eventually cause harm, it does not always lead to anorexia.

Nor does it seem usually to be related to past-life experiences, although it can be. I once had a client who went back to a life in ancient Rome, where she had been a man in a wealthy family. They had followed the Roman practice of feasting and deliberately vomiting to make room for more feasting. She had not come to see me for this problem, but when it surfaced in her past life, she recognized the pattern and told me she sometimes did this. Another client recalled a past life in which as a child she had been forced to eat large portions of rich, heavy food and was not allowed to leave the table until she had "cleaned her plate." She had felt stuffed after meals were over, and had resorted to vomiting to make herself comfortable. Although past lives are not always involved, overweight clients in general often go back to similar childhood experiences of being forced to eat too much, to clean a heaping plate, to leave nothing.

Another reason for gorging (but not purging) seems to be that the person came from a home in which food was scarce, and it was important to eat as much as possible before someone else got it. This can be part of the person's childhood or a past life. This was Jane's situation in her past life as Sally, described above, whose brother got the lion's share of the food. Although Jane was not a purger, she ate very fast and gorged on whatever food she could find. And she was obese.

Like obesity, gorging and purging seem to have various causes, not always related to past-life experiences. Furthermore, even if there is past-life experience, it may take some reinforcement from the present lifetime to develop into a full-blown problem.

Cravings for or aversions to particular foods seem to be more often caused by past-life experience. I think of John, who came for help with weight control. One of his problems was an uncontrollable craving for chocolate. Since his childhood, he had been unable to resist chocolate; as a young boy he would steal candy bars from stores and hide them in his room. Now as an adult he still had times of gorging on chocolate, and was never comfortable unless he had a few spare bars of candy in his car, his desk, and around his house.

John went back to a past life in the early years of this century, in which he had been a farmer in a Midwestern state. He had been caught in the hills during a blizzard, and wandered lost for hours through the blowing and deepening snow. He was sure he would not survive, but finally, miraculously, he had come to a farmhouse where they took him in, wrapped him in blankets, and gave him a cup of steaming cocoa. As he sipped it, he felt himself coming alive again, and he knew he would live after all. It was as if the chocolate was saving his life: "I felt my life come flowing back into me as I drank the cocoa." This was a profound experience, and he sat and wept helplessly with gratitude. John saw the connection with his craving for chocolate immediately, and the craving left him.

Aversion to a certain food is also sometimes connected to a past-life experience. This is not usually thought to be a "problem" worthy of therapy, as we all have some foods we like better than others and in our culture it is usually easy to avoid those we don't like. But the sources of food aversions do occasionally appear in past lives, as Dr. Hoffmann's client's aversion for eggs and egg salad did. And sometimes they appear even if they weren't being directly sought.

Mary, for example, had come for help with her weight problem, and I asked her Upper Mind if there were any past lives "connected with any food issues." I was thinking of fattening foods or overeating, of course, but her Upper Mind took me literally, as it always does. Her Upper Mind led us back into three past lives "connected with food issues," but only two were related to her weight problems.

In the third, Mary found herself a woman standing in a crude shack in front of a big black stove. Huge iron pots were steaming on the stove. Mary was taking hot beets from the boiling water in one pot and peeling them, then handing them to another woman who chopped them into the other steaming pot. Mary and the other woman were making borscht, apparently, or more likely a simpler kind of beet soup, and they were making a lot of it, for a large group of people. Despite the hot stove and the steam, a cold wind came through cracks in the walls of the shack, so the shack was drafty and cold, and Mary knew there was "endless" snow outside.

The two women were prisoners of an army, and beets were all there were to eat; it was the women's all-day job to make the beet soup for the whole camp. We never found out where or when this life was lived, but Mary knew she had been forcibly separated from her husband and children, who may have been killed, and that this would be the end of her life. She was depressed and hopeless, physically uncomfortable from the cold, hated every beet she peeled, and could barely swallow her share of the soup they made.

Mary laughed as she came out of this past life, and told me she had never been able to stand beets, and now she knew why. Obviously, her hatred of beets had nothing to do with her weight problem, but her Upper Mind had taken my direction literally and led us to a past life in which "food issues" were involved. I asked her if she thought she might like beets better after this. She said she really didn't care, but she had never had any problem avoiding them and might continue to do so. Or maybe she would try one, and see. It was clearly not a big issue for her, and why should it be?

Teresa's problem was a little more serious, as her aversion was to salad greens of all kinds and "slimy" foods such as cooked vegetables. These foods had always made her gag and she never ate them, with the result that her diet was seriously deficient in vegetables. Teresa also had a phobia for water and an intense horror of having anything brush over her face. She went back to a past life in which she had endured a particularly unpleasant death as a young girl. A nonswimmer, she had accidentally slipped into a deep, muddy pond and become entangled in the weeds and lily pad stems rising from the bottom of the pond. These had trapped her on the bottom no matter how she struggled to free herself, and she had drowned with the wet grasses wrapped around her head and face; in the process, she had swallowed some of the wet, slimy leaves.

It is easy to see how this dreadful experience had caused all three of Teresa's problems: her gagging reaction to salad greens and "slimy" cooked vegetables, her horror at having anything brush across her face, and her fear of water. She had come to therapy to find the causes of her gagging reaction, but in the process she also found the source of the other two problems.

Eating problems of all kinds may have their roots in past-life experience. They may also stem from experiences in this present lifetime, or from a combination of past-life experience reinforced by childhood experience. It is wise to ask the client's Upper Mind where the source of the problem is; it knows, and will lead the therapist and the client to it.

With most eating problems some supportive therapy is a good idea even after the person begins to eat normally. For one thing, eating "normally" is something many people with eating problems do not know how to do, and they need some instruction in basic nutrition. Also, it takes time to lose—or gain—weight, and an occasional session to reinforce the new eating habits and encourage the person to continue eating properly is a good idea. And finally, people with eating problems usually have very low self-esteem because of the problem itself. For a while, they need continuing support from the therapist, who knows their problem and that they are beating it, and who is on their side.

As we have seen, although not all eating problems have their roots in past lives, a good many do. A person who finds it unusually hard to lose weight and keep it off, or who was the "fat kid" of the family and has become a fat adult, or who has a tendency to gorge on certain foods, or who has a more serious eating disorder such as anorexia and/or bulimia, might want to find out if any past lives are involved and, if they are, examine them. In such cases, a good percentage of the problem seems to be defused, and the person can take control of his or her eating patterns much more easily and build new, healthy ones.

CHAPTER SIX

DEPRESSION AND OBSESSIVE-COMPULSIVE DISORDER

The terms "depression" and "obsessive-compulsive disorder" are really catchall words for sets of symptoms, and they have nothing to do with the actual causes of the conditions. When one looks at the causes, however, as one does in past-life or other regression therapies, those causes emerge as extremely specific and as stemming from particular situations. I will discuss depression first.

Officially, depression is only diagnosable as a disorder, "clinical depression," when it meets certain standards: The person will complain of lethargy, lack of interest in anything (including sex and food), difficulty sleeping, a general sense of being "out of it," and often, thoughts of suicide. These are some of the symptoms of severe clinical depression. Depression is no joke. As the numbers tell us, suicides rise every year, especially among the young and the elderly.

Yet even people who do not have enough symptoms to meet the "official" standard for clinical depression often have some of these symptoms. These people are only slightly depressed, going through their daily routines feeling trapped by their "duties," their work, their overall lifestyle. Life has become a treadmill to them, one they cannot get off.

There is one kind of depression that all of us experience at some time during our lives and that is not usually considered to require major, long-term treatment, although supportive therapy can help a lot. This is called a "reactive depression," and it is a natural reaction to the loss of someone who is important to us. Most people know that when a loved one dies, they will feel "depressed," and they realize that this is part of grief and loss and that they should be kind to themselves and let their grief take its normal course. Reactive depressions of this kind can also occur when we lose anything that is precious to us, such as a job or a beloved pet; people also get depressed in this way after a divorce, or after a child leaves home, or after a move to a strange place. Any loss can bring on a period of some level of depression.

To make themselves feel better, some people "self-medicate" with nicotine, caffeine, alcohol, or drugs; those with more serious forms of depression may take physician-prescribed drugs. The use of physician-prescribed antidepressant medications has skyrocketed in recent years; millions are spent each year on them.

Having said that, I will also say that comparatively few people come for past-life therapy for what they themselves call "depression," even though they have many of the symptoms. But most people fine-tune it more than that. They come for feelings of "loneliness," "isolation," "low self-esteem," "lack of self-confidence," "wondering what I am here for," "sadness," "trouble with my relationship," "not being able to find the right man (or woman)," feeling "bored all the time." The litany of unhappiness is endless, and it all translates to some level of depression.

Past-life therapy often helps with depression, but the causes of depression, of course, are not always in a past life. Bonnie is a good example. In her fifties, Bonnie had always struggled with slight feelings of "sadness." But she had been raised in Holland during World War II, when conditions were hard for her farm family, and she had explained her lifelong sense of loss as stemming from the difficulties of life during the war and from her move to the United States against her will after she married an American soldier. Her depression had deepened lately, after her two sons had left home: the older had married and moved away, and the younger had gone away to college in another state. Bonnie had begun to wonder what she was continuing her life for, now that her sons were grown. She had many of the classic symptoms above.

She had read somewhere that depression can have its roots in past lives, and had decided that this might be her case. But her Upper Mind said no, that her depression was not caused by any of her past lives but rather by something that had happened very early in her childhood in Holland.

We went back to when Bonnie was three years old. Bonnie had several older brothers, but she was the only daughter, and she was a happy little girl who followed her busy, cheerful mother everywhere and "helped" her with the household tasks. She tried hard to do these right, but sometimes she made mistakes that her mother would scold her for. But her mother loved her deeply, and they had a close, secure relationship. Bonnie, as the only girl, was her mother's special pet. Then one night, from her window, Bonnie saw her father drive her mother away in the farm wagon. She never saw her again.

Bonnie never had a chance to say goodbye to her mother, nor did anyone tell her where she had gone. Her beloved mother had simply vanished. The next morning her father was home as usual, and his sister, Bonnie's aunt, was there too, but no one told the children where their mother had gone, nor would anyone answer their questions.

They never did. In hypnosis, Bonnie recalled that she and her brothers had gone to the aunt's house for a few days, then come home again, and life went on as before except that their mother was gone. Their father was a dour, silent man even before this happened; for the rest of his life he refused to talk about it with anyone, including the children. Within months he had married again, a widow with two children of her own; he needed a woman to run his household and care for his children. Bonnie, of course, did not establish a close relationship with her, and did not even try to do so.

When Bonnie was in her teens, another aunt finally told her that her mother had died in childbirth when Bonnie was three: Bonnie's father had taken her to the local doctor, but he could not save her. It was the start of that trip to the doctor that Bonnie had watched from her window. But by the time Bonnie found all this out, in her teens, it was too late. She was already depressed, having decided as a tiny child that her mother had chosen to leave her, probably because she, Bonnie, had done something wrong. That's the way small children think, and by the time Bonnie found out the truth, that idea was firmly implanted in her basic belief systems and she didn't even know it.

It was this loss that Bonnie had been grieving all these years. She had no conscious memory of any of this, nor of her mother either, although she did know what her aunt had told her, that her mother had died in childbirth when she was three. But she had never put that together with her lifelong "sadness."

After her regression to this experience, Bonnie felt, and I agreed with her, that the loss of her mother was not in itself the full cause of her depression, but rather the way in which it was handled by her father and the other relatives. She could even understand it. The whole family, Bonnie said, was an unemotional lot, and work and a stiff upper lip were the main things for all of them. She also said that that Dutch farm culture cared little for the feelings of children; little children were to be seen but not heard, need not be told about adult matters, and did not go to funerals. Children worked, helped out as best they could, minded their manners, respected their elders, and at an early age boys began to support themselves and girls married some worthy farmer or tradesman and moved away. Bonnie, for years now a modern American wife, had long ago recognized the righteous rigidity of the culture in which she had grown up, but she had never put that together with her own feelings of depression.

After Bonnie regressed to this memory and understood the implications of it, she felt much more at peace. She felt more angry than depressed, angry at the "stupid" culture that had shaped the adults to be so oblivious to others' feelings, and particularly children's feelings. "Never lie to children" was one of the lessons Bonnie said she was taking away from remembering this experience. And there was also some lingering sadness, regrets for her father, who locked his own grief away so completely and never shared it with anyone, not even with his own children.

But in the end, Bonnie left it all "in the past," and in the process she found she could let her two sons get on with their own lives. She had been a good mother to them. After all, she had learned early from a master, her own mother, and she had almost unconsciously tried—successfully—to raise them as well as her mother had tried to raise her, even during the few years they had had together. However, Bonnie also saw that she had been trying to hold on to her sons; something in her had been afraid that if someone she loved left her, she would never see him again. But she also realized that her sons would always be her sons, wherever they were, and she could build adult relationships with them.

And perhaps most importantly, Bonnie realized that bad things happen, people die, but as long as truth is told, and grief is allowed, and people's feelings are acknowledged and expressed, grief can be borne and may even lead to new understandings.

Janet was another client whose depression was caused by an event that had occurred during early childhood, but in Janet's case, the event happened in a past-life childhood. Janet went back to a life during the Civil War, in which she, a little girl called Dolly, had died at the age of seven. But it was not this death that had caused the depression. Dying as a child in a past life seems not in itself to be related to any particular problem, depression or anything else, although the means of death can create problems.

About a year before Dolly died, when she was six, her beloved father was preparing to ride off to fight for the Union side, and Dolly and her mother were standing in the yard of their small farm home to see him off. Dolly was standing very near him, reaching up for a goodbye kiss, when two Confederate soldiers rode out of the woods, shot him dead, and rode away. Dolly's father fell against her; she screamed and shook him and had to be dragged off, covered in his blood, by her mother, as her father died.

Dolly was in a state of numb shock over this and she never recovered. She died a year later, at seven. Young as she was, she killed herself by wading out into the deep water of a pond, believing that she would then go to Heaven and find her father waiting for her. During the year before she died, Dolly never allowed herself to feel love or trust again. She felt numb, without feelings, and began to find solace in daydreaming about herself and her father in better days. She became more and more isolated from others, and she was not helped by her mother, who was silent, withdrawn, and consumed by her own grief for most of that year, and who neglected Dolly.

Janet had brought all of Dolly's feelings into her present life. Although we did not check this, this was probably not Janet's most recent life. There was a gap in time of about a hundred years between Dolly's death and Janet's birth. It is possible that she was also depressed in that intermediate life. Janet feels somewhat better knowing of her life as Dolly, but she still has occasional bouts of depression. But what may be important is that she can handle them better than she used to, and when she is ready, we will explore any other intervening life.

Kate, another client, went back to two past lives, both as men, that were related to her feelings of "isolation from others, numbness, feeling overwhelmed, and that tears were always just below the surface." The first life her Upper Mind took her to was in the early twentieth century, Kate's most recent life. She was Matt, an office worker in Detroit. Since his childhood, Matt had loved to write; it was his escape from his nagging mother; his silent, brooding father; and their continual fighting. He apparently had a real talent for writing and continued it as a hobby after he was grown, but he never attempted to publish anything or to use his talent except as a private pleasure.

When Matt was grown, he married; over the years he and his wife had two children. Matt was a good man, a good husband and father who supported his family as well as he could with a low-level office job. But he always felt "isolated from others, numb," as if nothing was quite real: as if he was only going through the motions of living. He created a strong fantasy life, more exciting than his real life, and he read widely. Matt felt cut off from the people around him by his own talent and his wider interests. He never stopped writing, and this was his secret joy, but he never tried to do anything with it either. When I asked him why, Matt said he wasn't good enough, and perhaps he wasn't. But the sad thing is that he never tried and so never really knew. Matt died in a car accident when he was forty-six, and after the death experience Matt said that he didn't really care that he had died. This life as Matt, Kate's most recent life, was the source of Kate's feelings of numbness and isolation.

The second past life that Kate's Upper Mind took her to was a life in the 1600s in Egypt as Ali, another male. This life was the source of Kate's feelings of being overwhelmed and that tears were always just below the surface. The relevant event happened when Ali was eighteen or nineteen.

Ali was inadvertently caught up in a mob of rebels determined to attack a town leader's house and kill him. The guards at the man's house brutally attacked the mob with clubs, killing and injuring many of the people. Ali was not hurt, but as he watched this happening and surveyed the courtyard littered with the dead and injured, many of whom he knew as good fellow townsmen and friends, he felt "overwhelmed" by the cruelty and his own sense of helplessness and hopelessness; his tears were indeed "close to the surface" and they could not be shed. Ali had also felt "overwhelmed" by the sheer physical power of the mob itself. He had not wanted to participate in the riot but he could not get out of the mob and they had simply carried him along with them. Later, Ali himself became some sort of official in the town, and when he was forty-three he was strangled in the street by a member of a rebellious faction who was angry with one of Ali's decisions.

These two past lives together were the sources of Kate's feelings of "isolation from others, numbness, feeling overwhelmed, and that tears were always just below the surface." This is a good example of the exactness of people's spontaneous descriptions of their symptoms: These were the words Kate herself used to describe her feelings at the beginning of the session. She did not say she was "depressed." I could have lumped these feelings together and written down "depression" in my notes for Kate, but I did not; I wrote her words down as she said them, and the two past lives that were related to those feelings were equally specific.

People do sometimes say they are "depressed." Both Bonnie and Janet used that word, because they had read of the symptoms of depression and recognized that they had many of those symptoms. And many people have been given that diagnosis by a doctor or a counselor before they ever seek past-life therapy. But the word "depression" can and usually does mask the exact causes. That is no problem for the Upper Mind, which finds the causes anyway, but when a person lists their feelings more exactly, one can see how very specifically they formed.

The causes of depression are always sad: depressing, in fact. One of the most tragic causes I have ever heard was Angie's. Angie gave her feelings specifically. She said that she had always felt that someone important to her was missing, some man, and as far back as she could remember, she had quickly scanned every crowd for this man. If she walked into a room, or down a street, or anywhere where people were gathered, her eyes did a fast involuntary scan of all the men, looking for someone. Yet she had no idea what this man would look like if she ever found him, or who he was, or why she wanted to find him, although she just "knew" she would know him if she ever did find him. When she didn't find him, as of course she never did, she felt sad and as if she might cry. Angie lived in this sadness, this slight depression, most of the time, a kind of grief with no apparent cause.

Her Upper Mind took her back into one of the worst tragedies of our century. When her magic chair stopped, she found herself a little girl of three or four peering through a wire fence across a bare yard. Every morning and evening she crouched at the fence to watch for a line of men who filed across the other side of the yard, going in one direction in the morning, the other direction at night. She watched for a particular man in the group: her father. When she found him, she waved; he was watching for her, too, because he always saw her, smiled at her, and lifted his hand in a small return wave. Then one evening he was not there, and he was never there again, morning or night, although she watched faithfully every day as the men filed by, scanning every head for that special one that was not there. Winter came, she caught some kind of illness, probably typhoid, and died there by the fence.

When I asked for the place of this little girl's death, the name that appeared on Angie's visualized screen was "Auschwitz." This explained everything, of course.

It was difficult for Angie to get very many other details of this past life. She remembered being with her mother for a while in a "dirty smelly place," but her mother got sick and died. After her mother was gone, women in the camp looked after Angie and saw to it that she at least had some food, but for the most part she wandered around the women's and children's barracks on her own. Angie said that she had an idea that she had first begun watching at the fence with her mother; she thought that perhaps some of the other women also watched at the fence, although she could not see them clearly. Apparently the men were in the men's barracks on the other side of the yard and were taken out to work each morning and brought back in the evening, and the women watched for their husbands, sons, and fathers.

Angie was still looking for her father from that past life. She had died looking for him and had apparently been born into her present life as Angie still looking for him. That little girl had never had a chance to say goodbye to either of her parents, so before I roused Angie, I directed her to go, as that little girl, to a beautiful place and bring the little girl's parents there too, so they could all say goodbye to each other. I always direct people to say the goodbyes they didn't get a chance to say and to clear up any other unfinished business after exploring a past life, but in Angie's case this was especially important. That little girl had no unfinished business as such, but saying goodbye to her father was something that she badly needed to do so she could let him go and stop looking for him everywhere.

After examining this past life, Angie, who was born about twenty years after this little girl's death, felt that a great load had been lifted from her shoulders. She knew whom she had been looking for all her life, and she also knew she need not and would not look for him any longer. He was on his path, she on hers, and Angie was content with that.

However, as we talked of this past life after Angie was fully awake, she said that she believed that it also explained the facts that her search for the man had always worsened as the winter approached and that her general sadness and sense of loss were greatest then. Her father had disappeared from the line of men in the fall, as the weather turned cold, and the little girl Angie had been had died cold, alone, and still searching for her father, in the cold of winter. As Angie talked, I realized that she was describing Seasonal Affective Disorder, a condition in which the sufferer feels increasingly depressed as the days shorten in the fall and winter. Angie had not told me of the seasonal nature of her problems before; she had not thought that this was of any special importance. But now as she spoke of this, it all made sense. She believed that she would no longer suffer from the "sadness" in the fall and winter, and she was right: she doesn't. Nor does she look for "the man" anymore.

Obsessive-Compulsive Disorder is another condition that is sometimes found to be related to a past life, usually only one. This is especially true when the obsession seems completely irrational. For example, a person may not be able to leave the house without innumerable trips back to be sure everything is turned off even though he knows that everything is fine; or a person may count everything to make sure that things are in even (or odd) numbers: pears in a bowl, steps she takes up a walk, buttons on a dress; or a person must always do a thing in a certain order even though this makes no sense, not even to her.

Sometimes these compulsions come from past-life experience. One woman had a compulsion to take everything out of her purse and repack it from time to time during the day, to make sure that she had everything she might need. She found that her compulsion stemmed from a lifetime as a Native American medicine woman, in which she had neglected to pack a certain herb in her medicine bag when her group was moving. Later, she needed it when a child was injured. The child died and she blamed herself, vowing never to forget to take everything she might need with her everywhere she went. A man with a compulsion for checking and rechecking locks before he left home, who would drive back home to be sure the door was locked even though he knew he had just checked it for the tenth time, traced this compulsion to a past life in which he had neglected to lock his doors and thieves had broken in while he was gone and killed his whole family.

Sometimes an obsession is for a person rather than an action. A year before she came to see me, Sally had broken up with her boyfriend of three years, Andy. By now, Andy was happily involved with another woman, but Sally could not get over him. Sally had agreed that they should end their relationship; there were many things about Andy that she had come to dislike, and with one part of her mind she felt well rid of him. So she could not understand why she thought of him constantly, watched for him wherever she went, and had begun to drive past his house as if by accident, looking for him. She had written him several notes on the pretext of asking for his help with one thing or another, and although she had not sent them, she was afraid she might do so at any time.

Sally went back to two past lives that were related to her obsession with Andy. The first we looked at was in the early years of the twentieth century, in Indiana, and it was Sally's most recent life. Sally was a woman, Patty, married to a man named Donald. They had a happy marriage, lived comfortably, and had two children.

Patty died in a car accident when she was thirty-four; her children were twelve and fourteen at that time. Because her life as Patty was cut short by the car accident, before she was born into her present life, Sally had made it a goal to "finish her life with Donald."

But as we examined this past life, Sally was not sure whether or not Andy was the same person as Donald or was just "similar" to him. She said they were both "young-looking, and they care about people, work hard, are concerned, get along with their families, but they are different in other ways." Furthermore, Sally had an intuitive sense that they were not the same person. So after we examined this past life, Sally was not even sure that Donald and Andy were one and the same person at all.

After we examined the second past life that her Upper Mind took her to, Sally's Upper Mind answered that question. In this life, a life in the 1800s in Vermont, her name was Beth, and again she had a good marriage and a comfortable life with her husband, Robert, their son, and a large extended family. Robert died of an illness when Beth was forty-two; she herself died at fifty, of an illness that made her "tired all the time." One thing she said she learned in this lifetime was that she had managed perfectly well without Robert after he had died.

After this life was explored, Sally was able to recognize the relationship between Donald, Robert, and Andy. Her Upper Mind told her that Andy was, as she had suspected, only similar to Donald, but that the similarity was what had attracted her to Andy in this life in the first place. After all, "finishing her life with Donald" had been one of Sally's goals for this lifetime, and because of their similarities, she had unconsciously mistaken Andy for Donald. However, she had never actually met the person Donald is now, whoever that might be.

It was Robert, from her earlier life in the 1800s, who was the same person as Andy; the same soul, one could say. But Sally also realized that she had no reason to be with him this time, nor he with her. She had managed well without him after he died in that 1800s life and she could manage now. It was as if they had met in their present lifetimes to share a few years and then go on their separate ways rather than make a lasting commitment.

Sally was comfortable with this insight; she stopped obsessing over Andy, and was able to let him "go on his way" and go on her own way, too. Perhaps someday she will meet the person Donald has become now, and if circumstances are right, she may be able to "finish her life with Donald," as she planned to do when she came into this present life. Or perhaps she won't. But Andy is not that person, and Sally has been able to let him go.

A young man, Dave, had a similar obsession. His girlfriend, Dawn, had left him several months ago, and he could not leave her alone. Like Sally, Dave had begun stalking, parking in front of Dawn's apartment building where he could watch her windows, and walking past the door of the building she worked in when she left work, hoping to meet her "by accident." He had begun to stop in at night spots where she went with her new boyfriend, and he recognized that he had an impulse to pick a fight with him. Dave realized that this behavior was obsessive and even illegal and could get him into trouble, but he said he could not stop it.

In his regression, Dave went back to two past lives. In the first we looked at, he was a Native American man named Talor (phonetically spelled) in the 1700s. Talor loved a girl but her father arranged another marriage for her; Talor felt cheated and humiliated and challenged the girl's new husband to a fight, which he lost. As he died, Talor vowed that he would never let another man take a girl away from him again.

Dave's second regression was to the 1800s, in a mountainous area of Europe. His name was Arturo. When he was a young man, two of the girls from his village were kidnapped by a gang, taken into the mountains, beaten, raped repeatedly, and finally killed. One of these girls was the girl Arturo loved and had hoped to marry, and apparently she returned his love. Along with the other men of the village, he had searched the mountain caves and other hidden areas, but by the time they found the girls, they were dead and the gang was long gone.

Arturo was grief-stricken, of course, and he felt extremely guilty about it. He believed he had had an obligation to protect his girl and that he had failed her. Arturo had been away when the kidnapping happened, but he believed that if he had been home, it would not have happened. Arturo never got over this. He later married someone else, and lived a long and good life, but he became overprotective of his wife and daughter and died believing that a real man should be ever alert for danger to "his women" and protect them from it.

After these two past lives had been examined, Dave realized that neither of these two past-life girls was his ex-girlfriend Dawn. In fact, his Upper Mind told him that he has no past-life bond with Dawn at all. But he also saw that he had picked up some archaic attitudes that were not relevant to his life today. Dawn's present boyfriend was no threat to her; indeed, Dave had liked the man before he began to take Dawn out. And Dave had not been humiliated by the breakup with Dawn. In fact, he admitted that in some ways he had felt a bit relieved when the relationship broke apart. Dave's Upper Mind told him to "live and let live, and get on with his own life," and Dave agreed that he could do this. I believe that Dave may still be a bit overprotective of "his woman" when he finds another one, but at least he is aware of this tendency in himself and where it comes from. His obsession and the stalking have stopped. And he is dating again.

Although both Sally and Dave had problems with a relationship, I have discussed them in this chapter because of the compulsive nature of those relationships, rather than in the next, the chapter on relationships per se. In their cases, their relationships had become obsessions.

Some cases of "hypochondria" may fall into this category of obsessions that have past-life causes. A person who is convinced, despite medical reassurances, that there is something wrong with some part of his body, or that some fatal disease is just around the corner and will get him eventually, may be unconsciously playing out a past-life drama in which he had an injury to that part of his body or died of the dreaded disease. Lana was convinced that there was something wrong with her left eye; over the years, every examination told her otherwise, but she was sure the doctors had missed something.

Lana came to therapy for a relationship problem with her husband, but in the past life she went back to, a male life, she found that during a battle, her head, face, and left eye had been seriously injured. Blinded, she had died painfully of that wound and her other injuries. The unconscious memory of this was lingering, so she just "knew" there was something wrong with her eye. As we examined this experience, Lana herself suddenly recognized where her fear had come from, and she could leave it in the past where it belonged.

As we see, depression and obsessions often seem to have their roots in past lives. Many clients who come for some other problem entirely find themselves in past-life situations that explain some obsession, as Lana did, and many clients report that after they examine some past life their feelings of sadness or depression have lifted, explained by the past life even though they had not come for therapy for this problem and were not consciously seeking the explanation there.

As I said above, terms like "depression" and "obsessive-compulsive disorder" are merely general diagnostic categories. They are labels, and many past-life therapists, like myself, try to avoid such labels at all. Clients have certain specific feelings, and it is the job of the regression therapist to help them find the roots of those feelings, whether in a past or the present life. Once those roots are found and understood, the feelings usually melt away like snow beneath the spring sun.

Unlike the situation with some other problems, supportive therapy does not usually seem to be necessary for these problems. Once the cause is recognized, the depression or obsession goes away, and the person has no trouble living without it. This is almost always true for obsessions, and usually for depression, too.

But one exception is when one element of the person's present life is in itself depressing. This can happen if a person is in a boring, dead-end job, or a bad relationship, or some other situation that does not go away by itself. But even these people, after finding the fundamental causes of their depression, find that they are able to deal with the depressing situations of the present better and with more self-assertion. It is as if the underlying depression had kept them drained of all energy, all sense of ability to do anything to improve their lives. Once this is lifted, they feel better about themselves and can act more wisely, and they do so. For them, some supportive therapy can help them make whatever change in their lives is necessary.

As a rule, behaviorist and cognitive therapies have not proven to be very effective with these problems, although in some cases behavior modification can help with compulsions. Insight therapy, in which the childhood causes are sought through talking and increasing understanding, can sometimes help some people, but a good many sessions are required and it is not usually very effective at actually eliminating the problem. Using regression to find and examine the actual causes of these problems, whether they are in the present lifetime or a past one, can often heal depression and compulsions rapidly and easily.

CHAPTER SEVEN

RELATIONSHIPS

In 1994 and 1995, Dr. Rabia Clark queried 136 experienced past-life therapists about their uses of past-life therapy, and she found that troubled relationships were the most common problem, phobias the second most common.

In past-life therapy, people often discover that a good or a bad relationship has its roots in a past life, and sometimes in more than one past life. Sometimes I ask the client during the regression if the person in the past life was really the same person, the same soul, or if there was just something about him or her that is similar to the person in the present relationship. The answers I get split about half and half between these two possibilities. Sometimes a client says that yes, it really is the same person; sometimes, it is something familiar about the present-life person that reminds him or her of the past-life person. We saw examples of each of these situations in Sally's two past lives that were related to her obsession with her ex-boyfriend, Andy, discussed in Chapter 6.

The word "soul mate" is used a great deal today. It is often taken to mean someone with whom we have shared at least one or more past lives, with the assumption that those past-life relationships were happy ones. The experience of meeting such a person from our past lives can be a powerful and positive one. Sometimes we meet someone we just seem to "know" immediately, at first meeting: A sort of "click" seems to happen inside ourselves the moment we meet the person, and if we have met a soul mate, the click is a positive, happy experience.

But one can also meet someone we seem to "know" instinctively but who frightens us. We get a click experience then, too, but it is not a pleasant one. We immediately feel frightened of the person or have a strong dislike for him or her. Sometimes this is so strong that it is a physical reaction, a tensing in the stomach, a feeling of weakness or even an anxiety attack.

"Click" experiences, positive or negative, are rare, but they do happen, and they may well mean that we really have just met someone we have known in a past life, and maybe in more than one past life. If you meet someone and the click happens, the best advice is to pay attention to it, whether it is positive or negative. If it is negative, follow your intuition and run. That may be a perfectly nice person, but if you get a negative click, he or she is not for you.

But even when it is a positive click, it does not always mean that you and this other person are destined to spend your lives together and be happy ever after. It may mean that, but it may not, too. You may have had one or more good past lives with the person, but this time you may both have other plans. Many people have such a click experience and initially believe they have found their soul mates, but in hypnosis they say they were just "checking in" with each other, like the very old friends they were. But both people have other goals for this lifetime. Perhaps we must actually avoid too many lives with the same person; that might make us too dependent upon each other.

A negative click feeling, one that frightens you or makes you instinctively dislike the other person, may indicate that although you have just met someone from one of your past lives, the past-life relationship was not a happy one, to put it mildly. The other person might have injured, betrayed, or even killed you, or harmed someone you loved in the past life. Or it could mean that you injured the other person and are still feeling guilty about it. You may even fear, unconsciously, that he or she is going to take revenge. You could be right, too: Forgiveness is not easy, and sometimes people do seem to be carrying an old grudge for a past-life injury, either physical or emotional. If they meet the person in the present life, revenge can become an unconscious obsession with them. People do seem to repeat many of the same relationship patterns over and over through several past lives.

And it doesn't even have to be the same person. Ned, a man in his late thirties, had a history of "loving and leaving" women. Ned had started many relationships, but no sooner did the woman begin to be serious about him than Ned backed away, ending the relationship abruptly and cruelly, hurting her. In his regression, we found that in his most recent life, during World War II, he had been betrayed by a woman he loved; she had voluntarily told the Nazis his whereabouts and he and his small resistance group had been captured, tortured, and killed as a result. Now in this lifetime, Ned had still not forgiven her. Unconsciously, he was paying her back over and over, betraying her as she had betrayed him, although he was consciously unaware of it.

However, when we discovered all this in his regression, his Upper Mind also told us that he had not even met that same woman this time, at least not so far! But the women he was attracted to and then betrayed this time were all similar to that other woman in some little way: her eyes, or the color of her hair, or her voice. That was enough for Ned's unconscious, focused on revenge as it was: This must be the same woman, she has the same eyes! So the ugly unconscious pattern repeated, over and over. In his regression, he had to forgive that other woman from that other lifetime, and he managed to do it once he saw the pattern.

In Ned's case, neither he nor the women he had loved and left so hurtfully seemed to have had any click feelings when they met, either positive or negative. After all, they had not known each other in any of their past lives. If he had met the woman who had really betrayed him in the past life, he (and she as well) might have had a strong negative click feeling. And who can tell what might eventually have happened? Fortunately, Ned has finally forgiven her, and is trying to build better relationships now.

In other words, like Ned, we sometimes do carry our grudges from one life to another, and we may unconsciously act on them, too, carrying out destructive patterns over and over that waste our own energy and hurt other people. The unconscious nature of such grudges may make them harder to get rid of, because consciously, we don't even know we have them. Yet just like anything else we carry into this life from our past lives, such a grudge can influence our actions.

The kinds of relationships people say they have had over the years with other people show a lot of switching about of "roles." For example, your mother in this life may have been your child in your last life and your good friend or your rival in still another lifetime. You and she may have changed genders from life to life; in fact, if you have lived very many lives together, you probably have. You may have actually chosen her as your mother this time because of good past-life connections. Or you may have chosen her because the two of you still have problems to work out, old scores to settle, perhaps. Or you may have had no past-life connections with her at all but with some other family member instead, or none with any of your family. But loving family relationships that come in from past lives can go rolling on over and over for generations, and they will be a source of strength and joy for the people involved.

If you have always had an especially strong feeling about some family member, and that feeling is returned, you may have known that family member in a past life and chosen to be reborn into his or her present family. Or you may be especially drawn to one particular child or grandchild: not exactly loving that child more than others, but a feeling that your relationship is different, special; that it has gone on for a long time. That child may have chosen to return to your family, to you. These inner knowings can make for loving and positive relationships between generations. If you have such a connection, it is rare and valuable, and should be treasured.

Sometimes a person has two positive click feelings about two different people. One woman, Angela, had married very young on the strength of her first positive click experience. She felt that she had met her soul mate, especially when she learned that her husband had had the same positive click experience when he met her. They were deeply in love when they married and they both expected to be happy, and at first they were. As time passed, however, Angela and her husband had a good many difficulties in the marriage, and over the years they grew farther and farther apart. Although they still loved each other, the passion had gone out of their relationship, and it was more of a "brother and sister love."

Then when Angela was in her early thirties she met another

man with whom she shared another strong positive click experience the moment they met. After great hesitation, they began an affair that had continued for two years when she came to see me. Angela felt increasingly guilty about betraying her husband and had come to the conclusion that she had to decide which of these two men she should be with. As she told me, she loved them both, and that was her problem.

In her regression, she discovered that she had known both of these men in two different past lives and had had good relationships with each of them. Angela and her present husband had had a close sister and brother relationship in a past life, but it had been marred by his insisting she stay at home so she could keep house for him, instead of marrying as she would have liked to do. As for Angela and her present lover, they had been married in another past life, and reasonably happily so. They were of reversed genders in that life, so that Angela had been the man and her present lover the woman.

But Angela's Upper Mind also told her that the relationship with her present husband was over. It was no longer good for either of them, although it had been good at the beginning, while they both "grew up." But now they both needed to break the old connection. They had become too dependent upon each other's presence. Her lover, according to her Upper Mind, was the person she should be with now. It was a more mature relationship and would allow both of them to grow, and, her Upper Mind hinted rather mysteriously, they had some old issues to work out between them. Just what these issues were, Angela's Upper Mind would not say.

In Angela's case, her Upper Mind said she had actually lived two different past lives with these two men, one with her husband and one with her lover. Julie had a different situation. Julie had a son with whom she had always had a stormy relationship; even as a little boy he had challenged every direction she gave him. He seemed to think he should be the boss, not Julie, his mother. And Julie was aware that she herself encouraged his behavior. She was a little afraid of him and often just "let him get away with it." He had been a cut-up in school and Julie had almost despaired of his future, but magically, so it seemed, when he reached his twenties and moved away from home, he suddenly became a responsible citizen, started his own successful business, married, and proceeded to build a stable family. But Julie's tension with him remained and they were not friends.

In hypnosis, Julie went back to two past lives that were relevant to her relationship with her son. In one, he seemed to have been her father, and a very strict one; in the other, he seemed to have been her teacher, and he was at least as strict. And in those past lives, Julie had been terrified of both of those men. Yet when I asked her Upper Mind whether or not these two men were really her son, her Upper Mind said no: She had never known her son in any past life. It seemed that he was just naturally bossy! Perhaps he had become that way in his own past lives. But it was this very bossiness that had reminded Julie's unconscious mind of those two men of whom she had been terrified in those two past lives, her father and her teacher in those lives. Her Upper Mind said that although the two of *them* were the same person, her son was not that person.

Furthermore, according to Julie's Upper Mind, she had not even met that man in this lifetime. Julie was greatly relieved about this, and hoped she would never meet him. I reminded her that there is no such thing as "never" but that the odds were probably against it. Just the same, I also suggested that she should watch out for a negative click! In the meantime, Julie thought that perhaps she could work out a friendlier, more adult relationship with her son, now that he is grown and independent and the unconscious fear she felt toward him is gone.

Sometimes relationship problems are not with any specific person but rather with either men or women. This was true for Ned, whom I discussed above, and Maria had similar problems: Every time a relationship seemed to be "getting somewhere," she would find some excuse to break it off. Unlike Ned, who unconsciously wanted to hurt women who reminded him of the woman who had betrayed him in his most recent past life, Maria broke off her relationships gently, trying to avoid hurting the man. Still, she broke them off and she knew that sometimes this was hurtful to him.

Maria went back to her two most recent past lives, in both of which she had been a very independent woman. In both lives, she had married "charming" men. But one of those charming men had died deeply in debt and left her almost penniless, with only the house left. She had had to turn it into a boarding house to earn a skimpy living for herself and her two children. In the other past life, she had been a pioneer farm woman in the West, and her charming husband turned out to be an irresponsible ne'er-do-well. In the regression, she commented wryly that the only thing he did well was drink. The burden of running the farm and raising their family fell entirely on her shoulders.

In both of these past lives, Maria had learned to do what she must to survive and she had managed very well, becoming capable and independent. But in the process, she had become suspicious of men, especially "charming" men, and she had brought this lesson into her present life with her. Since Maria was also attracted to such men and knew it, she avoided any deep involvement with them, although she did like to go out and have a good time. But if the relationship threatened to become serious, she broke it off. Maria knew she could do just fine by herself, and she was suspicious of the very men she was attracted to!

When she saw this pattern, Maria decided that she might look a little more deeply into the real characteristics of the men she went out with. Perhaps the "charm" wasn't always only skin-deep, after all. But perhaps she might also look around for men who were not so "charming." As she herself saw after her regressions, there are more important things than charm to recommend a man.

Some men seem afraid of even beginning a relationship with a woman, keeping clear of any commitment at all. Sometimes this problem has its source in past lives. Jack, a man in his forties, had never been able to establish a good relationship with a woman; he could never commit and never let a relationship go that far. Jack recalled three past lives in which he had rejected a woman who loved him.

One took place in ancient Egypt, in a life in which he was a young priest who had taken vows never to leave the temple or to marry. He and a young woman had fallen in love and had been meeting secretly; they planned to run away together. But at the last minute, he felt so guilty about breaking his vows that he changed his mind and failed to meet her at the prearranged place: In other words, he stood her up. He never saw her again. In the second of the past lives that we examined, he had been a "righteous" Victorian Englishman whose beloved sister had become pregnant; after he found out, he had nothing but scorn for her. He refused to have anything more to do with her, and she had to raise her baby in poverty and disgrace, without family help. In the third life, he was a man living in the Sahara about five centuries ago whose marriage was arranged by his family. At first he had loved his wife, but over time he came to hate her and he eventually left her, leaving her with their young child and knowing she would face the ridicule of the rest of their community and have a very hard time raising their child.

These three past lives show a pattern: rejecting women who loved, trusted, and needed him. Jack had carried a lot of unconscious guilt over these rejections, and now in this lifetime he had tried to protect himself from more guilt by refusing to even start any relationships. Through these three past lives, Jack saw that he was afraid that if he let himself build a relationship with a woman, he would eventually break it off, hurting her in the process. He was even afraid to let himself fall in love, or even to take the chance that he might: In these past lives, love had led to his deserting women he loved or had once loved. Having seen the pattern, Jack felt that he had let himself be stopped from relationships too long, and that he would be able to build a good one.

Neither Maria's nor Jack's relationship problems were directly connected with anyone they knew now, in their present lives. Instead, their relationships in their past lives had been so traumatic that they had become afraid to build any relationships at all with the opposite sex.

However, one other thing about their cases may be important. In all the past lives that had caused their relationship problems, they were both the same gender as they are now: Maria was a woman, Jack, a man. But in other past lives, both had experienced good love and marriage relationships when they themselves were the opposite gender. In two other past lives, Maria had been a responsible married man with a reasonably happy family, and Jack recalled two lives as a married woman in which he had been happy and had not deserted anyone. It is as if their troubles were specific to the genders they are now. In Maria's case, as a woman she could not trust "charming" men; in Jack's case, as a man if he let a woman reach his heart, he would end up rejecting and deserting her. But in those lives in which they were of the opposite genders, they had no such problems. But both of them could use the knowledge of the good relationships they had established in those other past lives to build on in their present lives.

Although both Maria and Jack were aware that their refusal to form relationships was a problem, neither felt any loneliness about this: They just felt that it was a problem, something to be solved. But many people do feel constant loneliness, and sometimes it has been caused by past-life experience, and often through no fault of their own.

Tony was a young man in his early twenties, and he felt himself to be alone wherever he was. And indeed, with no close friends and a dull job, his life was a daily routine that seemed to be going nowhere. Furthermore, girls seemed not even to notice him, and he had seldom dated. Tony struck me as very shy, too shy to assert himself enough to even get to know another person well, male or female. His attitude toward me was diffident: low voice and down-cast eyes, as if apologizing for being there and taking up my time.

Tony recalled two past lives in which he had been excluded from the community life. In one, in an ancient Greek village, he had been orphaned when he was ten or so. He had made himself useful by doing odd jobs, and although he was able to get enough to eat, no one particularly cared about him. He slept in stables, and "People look right through me," he said. He rarely spoke up about anything; if he did, no one seemed to hear him. In the second past life, he was raised in an abusive family in Pennsylvania, and he ran away in his teens and joined a wagon train that was heading west during the gold rush of 1849. He went with a prospector into the hills and helped him work a claim, but one day the prospector left and never came back. The boy simply stayed there alone in the hut they had built, sifting for gold but not finding any, until one day he was killed by a roving band of men, probably claim jumpers.

During that life Tony had learned not to trust other people: first, the people in his abusive family, and second, the other prospectors, many of whom were always ready to kill anyone they thought had actually found some gold. He had kept away from them as much as he could, but he was lonely in his hut after his prospector friend disappeared. And of course, in the end the other prospectors did kill him. In the Greek life, he was excluded from interactions with others except for the chores he did for them, and he knew there was no way he could improve things. He would always be lonely and alone. In both lives, he saw that others had friends and families, but he had none. And trying to relate to anyone in either life was dangerous. In the Greek life, he would be ignored or laughed at; in the other life, while he was with his family in Pennsylvania he learned to keep out of the way for fear of blows, and with the prospectors he didn't dare approach them for fear of what they might do to him.

Finding the sources of his loneliness was a help to Tony. He realized that conditions were different now, in this life, and he could dare to be more open with others. In fact, from the way his demeanor with me changed after we had examined those two past lives, I could tell that he would indeed become friendlier and less shy, displaying healthier self-assertion. His previously low voice was stronger and more inflected; his eyes looked at me instead of down at his clenched hands. In fact, his hands themselves were relaxed now.

But we also talked about the fact that making friends is always a bit chancy, and this is especially true when it comes to going out with girls. One can sometimes get hurt, no doubt about it. I recommended that he go slowly, even start by simply making a friend at work before he started asking girls to lunch. I also warned him that he should expect to make a few mistakes at first, and he should be ready to forgive himself for those mistakes.

I gave Tony all these warnings because, in cases like his, although the fear of approaching others in a friendly manner might be gone, he had not developed the social skills necessary to do this effectively. In other situations, like the ones above, merely being free of the problem is usually enough to allow the person to get on with his or her life. But in cases like Tony's, and especially when the person is young, some new social skills often need to be learned before the person can truly be free of the problem. It is best to warn people of this; that way, they won't plunge in too fast and get hurt. As I said in Chapter 4, it's all very well to get rid of your fear of water, but don't jump off the high dive until you learn to swim.

There is something else that needs to be said about relationships, and it is very important. As I have mentioned above, and throughout this book, people seem to live lives in both genders. If we have a more or less even split between male and female lives, we seem to be able to adjust to whatever gender we find ourselves this time. We will learn in our childhoods what our present society expects members of our present gender to be like, and we will adjust ourselves to that model as well as we can.

Yet we seem to take our experiences of being the other gender into our present life as well. It can make women more assertive than our society has approved of women being; it can make men gentler and more nurturing than is usually expected of men. We in the West live today in societies that are much more forgiving than past societies have been when it comes to gender behavior. Our Western societies are complicated and pluralistic, and they offer many different models of "correct" gender behavior. But the old stereotyped models still linger, and they often stop people from expressing their true selves or reaching the goals they came in with.

Yet we are all individuals, each with our own goals, abilities, and aspirations, developed partly over our past lifetimes and partly from our experiences in this life, and we do best when we recognize that fact. It affects ourselves and our relationships. Relationships can get into trouble when people accept the old stereotypes about what males and females are "supposed" to be like. It is best to realize that some people like to tinker with engines, others like to cook; and they can be female or male either way.

I guess that's the point. Men are not from warlike Mars, and women are not from loving Venus. We all have elements of each gender in our makeup, or we do if we have been lucky and lived a reasonable balance of female and male lives. A woman may much prefer to start and run a business and a man may just love cooking and prefer to stay home and do it. In fact, in our society, these role changes are becoming acceptable for more and more couples, because of the breakdown of the old stereotypes. But if people don't realize this, if they keep on expecting the old behaviors from each other or from themselves, they are stifling each other as well as themselves and they will find themselves—and their relationships—unhappy and in trouble.

Another area that involves relationships and gender identifications is the area of homosexuality, both male and female. Unfortunately, this is an area that is in much need of research into the past lives involved, because no research has been done and few if any cases have been published by other past-life therapists. Here I can only speak from my own experience with clients. Of course, most gay and lesbian people do not come for past-life therapy for their gender identification; why should they? These days, they do not usually feel that this is a *problem* for them. They come for other reasons, the same problems as others, and I often do not even know they are gay or lesbian. The question may not even arise, and in any case I do not usually ask clients' Upper Minds the cause of their gender identification. But if there is a pattern, it may have to do with the numbers of lives as each gender the person has lived. Doris, a lesbian living in a good relationship, wanted to recall all of her past lives; Carol, a heterosexual woman, did the same. (I discuss Carol's series in more detail in Chapter 12.)

Carol had lived nine male and five female lives, a fairly good balance, and had grown to adulthood in all but one, a male life. Doris, on the other hand, recalled thirteen female lives and only three as males, and those three were all very short. In those three male lives she had died at four, five, and fifteen, respectively. Doris recognized that she had never lived as an adult male and had no idea what life was like for them. She was actually afraid of men, and preferred the "safer" company of women, including her sexual relationships. She still does. As I said above, more research needs to be done about this issue.

An interesting question about gender issues is raised by transsexuals, who say, "I am in the wrong body." From the standpoint of past lives, this is a fascinating statement, and it could well be true, but unfortunately, no one has done the necessary research yet to determine the truth. It could be that a person, after a long series of lives as one gender, feels strange and "wrong" to find him- or herself suddenly born into the other. This seems reasonable, but as I say, the necessary research to find out has not yet been done.

Relationships, and our attitudes toward them, are strongly influenced by our past lives. After a few past lives, we have all experienced a variety of relationships, some good, some not so good, and we often expect or even create repetitions of those relationships in our present lives, as the people I discussed above did. This is complicated by the fact that we come into the world packed with individual traits from past lives: goals, hopes, plans, talents, experiences and expectations, traits that are strengthened or weakened by our upbringing and our family's values. Nowhere is this truer than with relationships. It is important to "know thyself," as Socrates said, and that includes knowing what expectations about relationships you have brought with you into this life. We can free ourselves of our unhappy relationships and build good ones, but only if we accept the unique individuality of each one of us.

Most mainstream theories of psychology hold that people are attracted to each other because of various resemblances to some other person, often a parent. This can be a positive or a negative resemblance: One can be attracted because of good qualities or not-so-good ones. Although these beliefs are not always supported by people's actual choices if you look only at the present life, they do seem to be true when you examine their past lives. People do seem to choose relationships because of some similarity to a person they have known in a past life, sometimes even with the same person. So where relationships are concerned, mainstream psychology may have the right answers, but they need to be extended to include our past lives as well as our present ones.

As I said above, relationship issues are the most common problem people seek past-life therapy for. Issues that have to be worked out are not usually the results of good relationships in past lives, although they can be. But they are usually the result of relationships that were unhappy in some way. Perhaps a strict Victorian husband dominated his wife to the point of controlling her life and has now been reborn; she may choose to come back as his sibling, thinking she can dominate him now. Or a woman may have been a neglectful or cruel mother in a past life. She may deliberately choose to come back as the child of one of her children because she feels she needs to learn how to be submissive or, less happily, because she still feels the need to dominate that person who was her child.

As to whether people actually resolve these negative issues in the present life, the answer is, usually, no, not without help. If anything, negative patterns seem to get worse over the years in cases like this. Like good relationship connections, bad ones can also go rolling on for generation after generation. Some have been going on for centuries. In past-life therapy, people often become aware of these negative connections, and can finally let them go. This frees them from having to focus on the "payback" and lets them begin to act upon whatever good goals they brought in with them, or find some new, better goals for themselves. No one is fated to continue repeating old destructive patterns over and over. But it may be necessary to recognize that we are doing just that before we can change and get out of any relationship traps we may have built for ourselves over our past lives.

CHAPTER EIGHT

ADDICTIONS AND HABITS

In this chapter we examine four common and serious addictions: tobacco, alcohol, drugs, and gambling, as well as, briefly, two milder addictions or habits. Other addictions and habits, when they are related to past lives, show patterns similar to the ones I discuss in this chapter.

It is certainly often possible to eliminate addictions without examining past lives, and without hypnosis at all. Many people with addictions are able to kick their habits either cold turkey or through one or another of the excellent programs and remedies that are available today. Hypnosis can help, but it is often unnecessary.

For some people, however, these methods don't work. Some people try everything they can find and still have no success, and they are the ones who come, almost in desperation, for hypnotherapy. "You are my last resort" is a phrase all hypnotherapists are very familiar with. Sometimes, hypnosis and hypnotic suggestion alone are enough, but sometimes they are not. If past lives are involved, and they often are in these "hard-core" cases, the past lives will probably have to be examined if the person is to be free of the addiction.

But simply examining the related past lives may not be enough. It will help, but for most addicts, ongoing supportive therapy in a group or in individual sessions is needed. This seems to be because the person has to learn some new skills: how to live and function well without the drug, tobacco, or alcohol. For gamblers, however, this kind of supportive therapy seems unnecessary, perhaps because stopping gambling does not require learning any particular new skills for living (unless you count the new skill of being able to pay one's bills!).

No one has done any research on these matters, but my own experience as a past-life therapist tells me that smoking seems to be connected with past lives only about half the time, but drug, alcohol, and gambling addictions more frequently are. An addiction to gambling, for example, is almost always connected with past lives, and while alcoholism seems often to be connected to experiences in past lives in which alcohol was used as a consolation, addictions to drugs are often connected with various past-life religious and/or healing practices that involved using drugs. So there is no one definition of "addiction" from the standpoint of the past-life experiences involved. Therefore, I will discuss these various addictions separately.

It is often said that smoking is the most widespread addiction in our society. However, there is reason to think that alcohol is at least a close runner-up. A good many people are addicted to alcohol who do not know it. They may finally realize it when they find themselves, some rainy night, driving miles out of their way looking for an open liquor store so they can buy a bottle of whatever it is they usually relax with in the evenings. Or if not then, they may begin to suspect something is wrong when they wrap the car around a tree. Typically, such a person will not decide he or she is an alcoholic; no, they "have a little problem with drinking sometimes." Their first reaction to this insight is usually to call a private therapist; since "of course" they are not alcoholics, "of course" they do not need groups like Alcoholics Anonymous (AA).

Now, years ago, my reaction when such a person called was to tell him that I would be happy to see him after he had joined AA and attended meetings for a month. Then, if he still needed help from me, he should call again and we would set up an appointment. The immediate response was usually a long silence, during which I became a mind reader and could clearly read his thoughts. I would wait for his next line, which was "But I'm not an alcoholic," at which I would congratulate him and suggest that that should make it easy for him to stop drinking immediately on his own.

Sometimes this worked: Some people did start to go to AA meet-ings, and some of them also called me in a month or so and came in for a little private help to augment their AA program. But a lot of people I never heard from or about again, and I began to realize that this tough talk of mine was not helping them. So I began to ac-cept them as clients, for one session, during which we could ex-plore the causes of their "little problem." During the session and face to face, after we had explored the causes in hypnosis, whether past lives or not, they were usually readier to admit that maybe they really were alcoholics, and a good many of them agreed to join AA, too. I kept the schedule of the local meetings in my desk so they couldn't get out of promising me.

Because whatever the causes of a person's alcoholism might be, in this life or a past one, becoming aware of the causes is not usu-ally enough to break the addiction. The person has usually been using alcohol for solace, for comfort, for escaping from unhappy situations, and he or she must learn to deal with those situations in more productive ways, and without alcohol. For this, groups such as AA are invaluable for a lot of reasons. They are ongoing, de-mand a commitment, encourage self-honesty and insight, and someone is always available to talk over problems as they arise. Furthermore, the person's efforts are praised and rewarded, and members are expected to help other members as well. And when it works, which it often does, eventually they learn to live their lives better without alcohol.

When past lives are connected with alcohol, we see alcohol used in ways that are similar to the ways that the addict uses it now, in this life. I think of Amy, a woman with a husband and two children, who had begun to drink sherry heavily while cooking dinner. She began to frequently burn the food, and one evening she fell asleep in the kitchen and almost burned the house down along with the chops. At that point, Amy realized that she might have a "little problem."

In her regression, Amy went back to two past lives that had caused her "problem." The first we examined was a life in the 1800s, in which she had lived a lonely life as a spinster seamstress in England. She worked alone for long hours and came back at night to a dreary rented room. While cooking her meager meal, she would drink gin, her one extravagance, and after her meal she would continue to drink until she fell asleep. She had no friends, no family, no love in her life. But when she drank, she would pretend that she was cooking for a happy family, the mythical happy family that, as the lonely years went by, she knew she would never have.

Amy recognized that although she herself was married and had children, she had begun to feel like that long-ago seamstress. She had begun to feel as if she was merely a household servant to her family. She also realized that she had done this to herself by trying so hard to make everything perfect, trying to create the perfect family that she, as that lonely woman so long ago, had dreamed of as she dozed in her gin-soaked haze. Like all families, Amy's family wasn't perfect, but her drinking helped her to pretend that it was, and that she was a happy housewife and mother, cooking for that perfect family that the seamstress never had.

That lonely seamstress was also an alcoholic, but her life was not Amy's only alcohol-related one. Amy also went back to another, earlier, life in which she had deliberately used alcohol to make herself feel better. This was a life as a man in Europe in the 1600s, who had been badly injured when he fell from a tree and who lived in constant pain from then on. He had used a kind of beer to assuage the pain, drinking it slowly but steadily all day. Whether or not he was also alcoholic we never learned for sure, but he never let his drinking go too far and never got seriously drunk. But it may have been in this life that Amy first learned to use alcohol to assuage pain and hopelessness, so that later, in her life as the lonely seamstress, she readily began to drink to make her loneliness more bearable.

It is most likely that all of us have used alcohol in one way or another in most of our past lives. After all, alcohol in its various forms is as ancient as the human race, and every culture has had its methods of making it. It has always been used for pain relief and other medical purposes as well as general conviviality and as a simple everyday beverage. It still is used for these purposes. So we have all been exposed to alcohol and probably benefited from it in our past lives. But it may be that it becomes addictive when we begin to use it to deny our personal woes instead of solving them, rather than using alcohol in whatever ways our culture approves.

Smoking seems to be another matter. It is related to past-life experience only about half the time; and when it is, it is sometimes connected with simple relaxation and sometimes with the rituals of religions. Harry, for example, was a fairly heavy smoker. He went back to a life in the 1600s in which he had come to America from England, settled a small farm in Virginia, and grown tobacco for his own use. He had a special pipe his wife had given him, one of a pair. She, too, smoked, and they enjoyed relaxing together in the evening, comfortably smoking their matching pipes. Or Molly, who went back to a life as a busy housewife and mother in Greece in the late 1800s. She had been a secret smoker who hid her habit from others, but she enjoyed her "little cigarettes" with her moments of quiet solitude at the end of her busy days.

For Harry and Molly, smoking was connected with simple relaxation in their past lives. But sometimes smoking is connected not to relaxation but to ritual or religious use. Ralph went back to a life as a Native American man who had begun to abuse the smoking of tobacco. In his group, tobacco was supposed to be used only for ritual and ceremony, and was thought to increase the tribe's power as a group. Ralph had begun to use it secretly, hoping to increase his own personal power. This was discovered, and as punishment he was forbidden to use tobacco for any purpose. Ralph may have lived another, earlier, life in which tobacco played a major part, because it sounded as if he already had a tendency toward tobacco addiction in that Native American lifetime. But if he did, we did not find it.

Of these three people, only Ralph successfully kicked his smoking habit after examining his past life and without supportive therapy. The other two, Harry and Molly, needed one more session of additional hypnotic suggestions to be completely free of their smoking addictions.

Chewing tobacco is sometimes related to past lives, too. Fran, in her midtwenties when she came for help, had begun to chew tobacco in her early teen years, and she was thoroughly addicted to it. She had tried to stop many times, always unsuccessfully. Fran went back to a past life as a girl who died at fifteen in a prairie fire in the 1700s. Her father grew a small crop of tobacco and the young girl enjoyed chewing the leaves, as did the whole family. In Fran's case, exploring this one past life, the only one related to her addiction, was exactly what she needed: She stopped chewing tobacco that very day, three years ago, and has not started again, nor has she begun to use tobacco in any other form.

This immediate success is rare for hard-core tobacco addicts. Perhaps one difference was that Fran's habit was chewing tobacco rather than smoking it; another difference may be that her one past life related to her addiction was two centuries ago. But with hard-core smokers like Harry and Molly, merely examining the related past lives helps but it is not usually enough. They also need other hypnotic suggestions and sometimes some supportive sessions as well to successfully kick the habit and keep it kicked.

But one should remember that it is usually only the hard-core smokers who come to a private therapist for a smoking addiction at all. They have tried hard to stop on their own, before they ever come to a therapist, and they have usually tried various programs, patches, gum, acupuncture, everything they can find before they come. With a less addicted smoker, and when no past lives are involved, it is often possible to eliminate the addiction in one or two sessions with hypnotic suggestions only, but this is not enough for these hard-core smokers with past-life involvement.

Drug addictions are often related to past lives, and they are usually connected with some ritual or healing use of drugs. Ginny, for example, who was addicted to marijuana, went back to a life as a medicine woman in a Native American group in the 1600s. She had smoked some kind of mind-altering herb to assist her in her healing duties. She lived a long life, and toward the end of it she was unable to cure an illness that decimated the tribe; her own daughter and grandson died of this illness. She herself survived, but she believed that her healing skills no longer had any power to help her people. This depressed her so much that she began to chew and smoke herbs simply to comfort herself. One day she wandered away from her tribe while gathering herbs and died (probably of a heart attack) in a drug-induced haze, an "old woman."

After we examined this past life, Ginny realized that she herself felt useless to her family; she felt as if no one needed or wanted anything she could do. This was very depressing to her, but when she smoked marijuana, she left those feelings behind: they didn't matter anymore. The old medicine woman had used her herbs for exactly the same reason. Ginny saw this, but she needed time to establish herself as a valuable member of her family, and she had to become more assertive to do that and more aware of her true skills than she was. All this required insight and work on her part as she learned a new way to live and relate to her family members and friends. But she made it, and stopped her marijuana smoking.

Sam, a cocaine user, also went back to a life in a primitive group. In that life he had contracted a painful illness, probably caused by a parasite, and his only relief was through chewing a tree bark that numbed the pain. He chewed the bark constantly, dying finally of the disease and still feeling numb from the bark. Now in this present life, Sam sought release from his troubles through drugs, at first with marijuana, then cocaine. Like Ginny, although exploring this past life helped him stop using cocaine, Sam had to learn to deal with his troubles in more productive ways. For Sam, group sessions gave him the support he needed.

Gambling is an addiction that is probably increasing in the United States. People who have developed a taste for gambling in past lives may enjoy placing a small bet on an occasional game of bingo, a card game with friends, or a day at the races, but this may not become a serious problem unless and until a socially acceptable gambling opportunity with really big stakes presents itself. In recent years, state-sponsored lotteries, offtrack betting offices, and large gambling casinos have provided those opportunities, and the rise in clients who come for addictions to gambling is noticeable. Since my state sponsors lotteries and offtrack betting, and since my office is within a few miles of a large gambling casino that opened four years ago, I now see a fair number of gambling addicts, whereas in the past I might have seen less than half a dozen a year. One sign of the times is that our little town now sports a brand new chapter of Gamblers Anonymous.

Most of these people say that until recently they contented themselves with occasional card games with buddies, or joining in the office baseball pool, or playing bingo at the church every week. Although they enjoyed gambling, it was not out of hand and they were sensible about it. One would think that they could take advantage of their new opportunities to gamble and keep it within bounds as most people do, but gambling addicts seem not to be able to do that.

It may be that these new gambling centers seem so respectable. They are also legal, and to judge by the gambling addicts I have worked with, they are not people who want to break laws and will not do so to gamble, or not very much. Once gambling becomes legal and socially acceptable, however, they will gamble to the allowable limit. One might say that a gambling addict will gamble at whatever level the law allows, but not much further. If nothing but church bingo games are legal, they will content themselves with that. If thousands of dollars can change hands in five minutes at a *chemin de fer* table at a glitzy casino, they will be there, with the mortgage money ready in their hands.

Caroline had a serious problem with gambling. She had always enjoyed buying lottery tickets, spending perhaps ten dollars a week on them, often losing but sometimes winning small amounts. And as any gambling addict can tell you, the trouble with gambling is that sometimes you win. But since the new casino opened, Caroline had begun to stop there after work each evening; her husband's work as a long-distance truck driver took him away from home for days at a time, and she was now spending all of her spare time at the casino. Caroline was frightened because she had lost so much money; her husband knew nothing of her gambling, but she knew she would have to tell him soon because the debts were piling up very fast.

In her regression, Caroline went back to three past lives connected with her gambling addiction. In the earliest, she was a boy, Tim, who died at sixteen in 1840. Tim's mother had died when he was very young and Tim lived with his father on a small boat on the Mississippi River. His father did various odd jobs as they traveled along, but his main source of income was gambling, playing cards with other men on bigger boats or in bars and clubs on shore. As Tim grew older, he himself often joined in the games, which he was good at and enjoyed. Tim died when his father got into a fight with another man during a card game and either fell or was pushed into the river; Tim jumped in to help him and they were both swept away by the current and drowned.

In the second of the three past lives, Caroline was a woman, Emma, living in the late 1800s. Emma was a prostitute in a rough club, probably in Chicago, and like the other women, she had a "special" guy. Her special guy played cards with other men, and Emma and the other young women looked on, making their own small bets on their "guys." When her guy won, he bought Emma presents with his winnings. Emma died at twenty-seven in 1880 in Illinois, probably in Chicago, in childbirth.

In the third past life related to gambling, Caroline went back to a life as Betsy, a woman who died at forty-two in 1926 in Ohio. Betsy and her husband raised horses. They raced them locally and bet on them, and they often won. Her husband was killed when he was thrown from a horse, and after that although Betsy continued to raise her horses, she no longer raced them. However, she loved to ride and rode to exercise the horses every day. She sold them to other racing people, and thus added to her income. But even without this she was not badly off, as her husband had left her well provided for.

Betsy's husband's friends remained polite after his death and invited her to some of their frequent parties, but they never included her in most of their activities, and even at the parties she felt she was considered to be not quite part of the group anymore. She watched the others play cards for money and wished she could join them as she and her husband had done, but she felt she could not because she had no partner and the others had not invited her to play. (After the regression, Caroline speculated that they might have "overlooked" Betsy because they did not want to embarrass her. They played for high stakes, and they may have thought that she, as a widow, was short of money. But at the time Betsy just felt excluded and longed to join in the card games and the gambling.) Betsy died from a fall from her horse, when she was forty-two, in 1926.

These three past lives may have been Caroline's last three lives before she was born as Caroline. They were certainly consecutive, three in a row. Tim was born in 1824 and died in 1840; Emma was born in 1853 and died in 1880, and Betsy was born in 1884 and died in 1926. Caroline herself was born in 1967, which leaves a gap in time of forty-one years after her Betsy life, so she may have lived another life between her life as Betsy and her present one. But if she did, that life had nothing to do with gambling. That addiction, according to her Upper Mind, had been caused by these three consecutive past lives and no others.

In Caroline's case, and in most gambling addictions, more than one past life is involved, but once they are examined, the urge to gamble seems to melt away. It has for her. However, perhaps to "play it safe," as gamblers say, before I woke her, I gave Caroline some direct hypnotic suggestions that she hated the whole gambling scene and considered people who were hooked on gambling sad, lonely people, and similar supportive ideas. These probably helped her to lose interest in gambling, which is essentially what happened. But with the other addictions discussed in this chapter, alcoholism, smoking, and drug use, although I always give appropriate hypnotic suggestions, some ongoing group or individual sessions are often required. For gamblers, continued support sessions seem not to be necessary.

There are other addictions that are often related to past lives, less damaging ones than the four above. In Chapter 5, I described the past life that had caused John's craving for chocolate; at the beginning of our sessions, John actually said he was "addicted" to chocolate. As I said, he went back to a past life in the early years of this century when he was lost in a blizzard. He miraculously stumbled upon a farmhouse, and the people there took him in, half-frozen and shaking, unable even to speak. They wrapped him in blankets and gave him a cup of hot cocoa in their warm kitchen. This, he felt, saved his life: "I felt my life came flowing back into me as I drank the cocoa." This was John's most recent life; it is easy to see why he was "addicted" to chocolate! He came out of this past-life regression with the decision that "chocolate is nice but not necessary anymore." Such strong cravings for foods, especially for sweets or chocolate, can often amount to addictions.

Bad habits sometimes take on the compelling character of addictions. Nail-biting is such a habit. It can be irresistible, and the nail-biter tries everything to stop but to no avail. Most nail-biters are intensely ashamed of the habit. They hide their hands, thinking everyone else will notice their nibbled finger ends and lose respect for them.

Dorothy had bitten her nails since childhood, and she had tried every trick she had heard of to stop. In her regression, she went back to a life as a busy farm woman in Ohio in the 1800s. She had a garden, as everyone did, and since she took good care of it, she always had dirt under her nails. Furthermore, her nails were always somewhat broken and ragged from the farm and garden work. The dirt never all came out no matter how she scrubbed, and the

ragged edges were invitations to picking at her nails. She would
nibble at her nails to get the dirt out and pick at the ragged edges,
finally biting the nails down to the quick. Now, in her present life,
whenever Dorothy saw the slightest hint of anything under a nail or
felt a ragged edge, she immediately bit it short, sometimes without
even realizing she was doing it. Examining this past life helped
Dorothy to break the habit, and although she occasionally still nib-
bles a bit at a ragged edge, she immediately realizes when she is
doing this and files it smooth instead. She has been able to let her
nails grow, and takes good care of them.

Habits such as these do not always have their roots in past lives,
although they often do. But if you have such a habit that is so compelling that you could call it an addiction, have had it since childhood, and have tried to break it without success, it may have begun
in one of your past lives.

Addictions, major or minor, should be suspected of having past-
life roots when they start very early in life (such as a smoker who
began to smoke at five) or when they seem impossible to eliminate
no matter what the person tries. Another clue to a past-life cause
may be that the person feels a sense of comfortable familiarity the
first time he or she tries the addictive substance. Many people, the
first time they try smoking, alcohol, or drugs, react negatively. It
makes them feel sick or faint, or tastes terrible to them. They may
go on to become addicted to it anyway because it seems sharp or
cool or the sophisticated thing to do, but their first reaction was
that they didn't like it. People with past-life connections to addictions, however, usually say that they knew this was "right" for them
the very first time they tried it. One man, who had secretly started
smoking at seven, told me it was as if he had been waiting for tobacco since he was born. And he was right—he had been, as it
turned out.

As I said above, not all addictions are related to past lives. Some
have been developed in this present life only, although they are
probably not the hard-core addictions described above. But in that
case, we can surmise that unless they are healed, the person may
well carry them on into his or her next life. And with tobacco,
drug, and alcohol addictions, whether past lives are involved or
not, various chemical effects in the brain are undoubtedly part of

the addiction, as the current theories hold. This may be one reason why ongoing, supportive therapy of some kind is necessary for so many addicts. But if past lives are involved, examining them can help the addict to kick the habit. Supportive therapy of some kind may also be useful or even necessary, but the process of getting rid of the addiction will be much easier after the past-life causes are explored and "left in the past," where they belong.

CHAPTER NINE

PHYSICAL SYMPTOMS

We seem to have two diverging streams of public opinion about the so-called medical model of health care today. One group, probably in the majority and certainly the "establishment," believes that the miracles of modern medicine can and eventually will save us all from disease and even from aging and perhaps from death itself. The other group, a minority, and definitely not the "establishment," is somewhat disenchanted with modern medicine and is exploring numerous alternative therapies, including past-life therapy. This second group is growing every year, but they are still a minority and so far there is little research to support most of the alternative therapies they embrace so hopefully. However, as soon as a reasonable amount of research does support such a therapy, it is apt to move into the more mainstream, establishment camp. Recent examples of therapies that have done this are acupuncture and biofeedback, not to mention hypnosis itself! Not very long ago, all of these were "alternative" therapies.

Those who disparage modern medicine should reflect on their own histories. Probably most of us are alive today because of modern medicine. I myself would have died at seventeen from a ruptured appendix if not for modern medicine, and a good many other people, with a moment's thought, must make similar statements. So this chapter is not intended as a polemic against modern medicine: it is one of the great wonders of our time, and we should all recognize that.

At the same time, there are some conditions that modern medicine does not seem to be able to help, and some medications that are associated with such unpleasant or dangerous side effects that people hesitate to take them. But when we have physical aches and pains we usually look first for physical remedies. People with backaches or headaches or sinus problems usually deal with them by taking some analgesic such as aspirin or an antihistamine. If the problem is severe enough, they go to a doctor, who prescribes a suitable medication or perhaps a healthier eating or exercise regimen. Sometimes this approach is exactly right: a good many physical problems have physical causes and are best eliminated at that level. But sometimes these approaches are not effective, and in those cases the causes may lie deeper, sometimes in a past-life experience.

From what we see in most past-life regressions, the physical problems that are carried forward from past lives seem to be the seemingly minor but recurrent problems, the ones with no apparent physical cause, the backaches and headaches and allergies that plague so many. This is probably because few past-life therapists work with the more major illnesses. But although the really serious illnesses and diseases are not usually thought to stem from past lives, there are a few therapists' case reports of healing, or at least remission, of such diseases as cancer, diabetes, and arthritis, when past-life therapy was used as an adjunct to modern medical treatment. And the two recent studies by Ronald van der Maesen in the Netherlands (mentioned in Chapter 3) indicate that past-life therapy is often helpful in eliminating the involuntary tics and gestures of Tourette's syndrome and in alleviating the hallucinated voices of schizophrenics and others with severe psychiatric disorders. These are important findings, and they suggest that some serious illnesses and conditions may be at least partially caused by past-life experiences.

Another major disorder that has sometimes been found to have connections with past lives is dissociative identity disorder, or DID (formerly known as multiple personality disorder, a better term). When DID has past-life connections, it seems as if a past-life personality has become invasive and is "taking over" the present personality from time to time.

But no one with a major illness should think that past-life regression alone is going to heal it. Here the miracles of modern medicine are essential. However, it is possible that even with a major illness, there is sometimes a past-life connection, and in such cases past-life therapy may help the modern treatment do its job. And the more minor problems do often disappear like magic after the past-life causes are examined in regression.

And sometimes the causes are to be found in two places: a physical cause in the present life and some experience that took place in a past life. Elsbeth, for example, had always suffered from minor backaches; they seemed to have no particular cause that the doctor could find, but they were not severe enough to slow her down. But then in her forties they became much worse. Her doctor, after extensive tests, could still find nothing wrong with her back, but he did tell her that she should lose thirty-five pounds and take the strain of all that extra weight off her spine.

Elsbeth set to work and lost some weight. Her back improved mightily, and so did her looks and her self-esteem and probably her health in general. But the backaches did not entirely disappear; instead, they went back to the old, familiar, low nuisance level at which they had been before she gained all that extra weight. Elsbeth came for past-life therapy to help her with her continuing weight problem, but she found the past-life cause of her lifelong backaches, too.

In one of the two past lives we examined, Elsbeth found herself a small brown boy shinnying up a palm tree to get coconuts and throw them down. He slipped and fell, wrenching his back as he tried unsuccessfully to cling to the tree trunk; he landed on his back on one of the hard coconut shells that littered the ground beneath the tree. His back was injured, but Elsbeth said that she felt that it was not the fall that had really injured the boy; it was the well-meaning attempts of his family and the other villagers to wrench his back around, trying to heal it, that had done the most damage. Even as that boy, in that lifetime, Elsbeth felt that if they simply left his back alone, it would be fine. But they tried to heal it in their rough ways, and that little boy never recovered from that injury and walked stooped over for the rest of his life. He also became obese because he was unable to get enough exercise. After Elsbeth examined this past life, her backaches faded to insignificance, and her weight problem was partially explained too.

A good many recurrent backaches are related to past-life injuries, usually exacerbated, like Elsbeth's, by overweight or lack of exercise in this present lifetime. Recurrent headaches are also frequently related to past-life events, usually a death experience.

Donna suffered from severe recurrent headaches every week or so, and she took physician-prescribed medication for them with only mediocre results. In regression she went back to a past life as Else in the 1700s in a small European city. Else's family was very poor, living in what we today would consider extreme squalor. One day, when Else was fifteen and alone at home, two men came to the house to steal whatever they might find. They apparently expected the house to be empty and were startled to find Else there, but they dragged her away with them and attempted to rape her. She struggled and in the process one of the men hit her on the head with a rock; this killed her.

Penny, another client who suffered from recurrent headaches, also died from a head injury as a girl child in a past life. In a primitive life in a South American tribe, she was running through the woods to escape a marauder when she stumbled and fell, striking her head on exposed tree roots and dying. Both Donna and Penny had brought their headaches into this life from the past ones, and whenever they were triggered by some minor event, they had the headaches. For both, after they became aware of the past life causes, the headaches disappeared; it was not necessary to search for the triggering events, and we did not do so.

Both Donna and Penny had suffered fatal head injuries in a past-life childhood. But the head injury that causes a recurrent headache is not always sustained in a past-life childhood. Ernie also suffered from recurrent headaches, and in the relevant past life he died as an adult by falling off a rocky cliff into water, hitting his head on rocks on the way down. Ernie had not actually died from the head injury; rather, he had fallen into the water and drowned, but he had been confused and only half-conscious after the head blow and in any case he was unable to swim. Ernie had come for help with his phobias for water and heights, and that past life was the cause of both of those phobias. Falling off the cliff was responsible for his height phobia, and drowning was the cause of his phobia for water. But as he died in that past-life regression, Ernie himself recognized that the pain he felt when his head struck the rocks was the same pain he felt when he had one of his lifelong headaches, and he himself identified that experience as the cause of the headaches. Perhaps it was: he has been free of them since that regression, and of the two phobias too.

I have used the word "recurrent" to describe the headaches of the three clients above, although they had all been diagnosed as having "migraines." There are considered to be four basic kinds of recurrent headaches: migraine headaches, tension headaches, cluster headaches, and headaches caused by a serious organic problem such as a tumor. Of these, the last can be accurately diagnosed by examinations of the brain itself with modern technology. There is probably no past-life cause for a tumor-caused headache. But the other three categories, migraines, tension headaches, and cluster headaches, sometimes have past-life roots. Any of these may turn out to be caused by a head injury in a past life, and this injury is usually associated with some traumatic death.

Melissa had more extensive headaches than these, and they were not only headaches. Melissa had suffered all her life from stiffness in her neck, jaws, shoulders, and upper back, as well as headaches, but during her teens these became much worse, real pain, not just stiffness and slight pain. Melissa was in her thirties when we worked together. She had lived with severe pain since her teens, although extensive tests had revealed no physical problem, and no medication or exercise seemed to relieve it. Melissa went back to four past lives that had caused all these problems. According to her Upper Mind, Melissa had lived twenty-eight past lives in all, so four out of that number was not an unexpected number to have caused her serious problems.

The earliest of the four lives we explored was in the ninth century in southern Europe. Melissa was a woman whose mother was considered a seer who could foretell the proper planting time for the "gardens." But one year the gardens did not grow well, and her mother had been beheaded as an "evil seer"; this was apparently the penalty for this failing. Melissa herself inherited her mother's function, and when one year, when she was twenty-five, the gardens did not grow properly, she herself was beheaded. The pain of this had contributed to her neck and head pain.

The next life Melissa lived that was associated with her pain was a male life in the early seventeenth century, in a village in England.

As a little boy of eleven, Melissa was playing in a field with another child, a little girl, and when the girl said she was hungry, the boy (Melissa) picked "something" up from the ground and gave it to her to eat. Soon the girl became violently ill, ran home, vomited heavily, and eventually died. Melissa could not see clearly just what the little boy had given the girl to eat, but felt that it might have been mushrooms. The little boy had not meant to hurt the girl and was terrified at the result, but men came to his home and dragged him away. He was charged with deliberately killing the girl and was beheaded, the penalty in that time and place for murder, even by a child.

The next pain-associated life for Melissa was in New England in the late 1600s and early 1700s, and was the life immediately following the one above, in England. This was a female life, and she was probably not entirely psychologically healthy. In her teens she "foretold" a house fire that actually occurred; later, Melissa thought it possible that she herself had started it. It is certain that the townspeople suspected that she might have started it, and they suspected she was a witch as well. She was placed in the stocks as punishment, apparently for a long time, and the cramping of her neck, jaw, shoulders, and back was excruciating. She never forgot this experience and became increasingly hostile, secretive, and isolated. Eventually she came to believe that she *was* a witch, and when she was about thirty, she was hanged for that or for something else; that is not clear. But Melissa's Upper Mind said that this hanging had little to do with the pain problems; the experience of being in the stocks was "much worse," and was especially relevant to her jaw pain.

In Melissa's fourth life associated with her pain, she was a woman living in the late 1700s; this was the life immediately after the New England life above. Raised in Italy in a farm family, when she was still a child her father was arrested and killed for stealing pigs and the rest of the family was thrown off their farm and driven out of the area. They wandered for a bit, finally meeting other wanderers, and made their way into France, where they lived by dancing, doing tricks, and probably stealing as well. It sounds a little like a gypsy life, although Melissa did not use that word. When she was twenty, Melissa stole a necklace and a bracelet. She was caught and beaten severely. The beating stripped the skin off her back and shoulders; she lost consciousness from the pain and died there in the dirt of the village square.

All of these experiences had contributed to Melissa's headaches and her neck, jaw, shoulder, and back pain, of course. But the last of them had occurred almost two centuries ago, and she had lived other lives since then. Although the slight stiffness Melissa had felt since childhood could be explained by these long-ago past-life experiences, they were *so* long ago that it was surprising that they could have caused such severe current pain problems by themselves. And they had not: there was a trigger experience, an event in her present life that had set all these problems off like the primed gun I spoke of before.

When Melissa was in her teens, she had had a summer job as an aide at a hospital for the mentally ill. Because of her youth and her lack of training, she had worked in an office and had not been allowed to actually work with the patients, but one day a patient had made his way to the office and grabbed Melissa by the neck and shoulders. He had been immediately pulled off by the staff, and although Melissa had been frightened, she had not been hurt, but that had been enough to trigger all those past-life memories and change her lifelong sense of stiffness to real pain. Melissa remembered this experience consciously, and after her session she herself recognized it as the trigger for all those past-life experiences.

There had been no physical damage done in the attack by the patient—doctors had attested to that—but Melissa had suffered a great deal of pain ever since, as if there had been severe physical damage. Terrifying as such an experience might be, most of us would have come through such an attack with no long-lasting physical symptoms. But in Melissa's case, the attack acted as a trigger, recalling to her memory all those past-life experiences of pain in her head, jaws, neck, shoulders, and back. And in Melissa's case, it was probably important to identify the trigger and recognize it for what it was: a trigger for the past-life experiences. Once they were triggered by the attack in her teens, all the pain of those old experiences came back to Melissa's body. But once the past-life causes were explored, her pain could be "left in the past," where it belonged.

A good many allergies are found to have come from past-life experiences. Bill had allergies to grass, clover, and the smell of mud; he traced these to a past life in which he, as a terrified little boy, had hidden from invaders by crouching against a muddy riverbank with his face buried in the grass and clover that grew there. As he listened to the screams and the sounds of killing coming from the village, he sobbed for his parents and from fear. He was soon found by the invaders and killed. Grass, mud, and clover had become associated with his fear and his desperate crying. In a sense, his body was reacting to grass, mud, and clover by "crying" again: his sinuses filled and his eyes teared, as they had while he had crouched sobbing in terror against the muddy riverbank so long ago.

Bill's allergy was related to a death experience, although it was his fear and sobs of terror that had caused the allergy, not the death itself. But not all allergies are related to death experiences. Alissa also had an allergy to grass, especially the smell of crushed or fresh-mown grass. She went back to a past life in Wales in which she had been raped at fifteen in a field where she had been watching her family's sheep. The man had forced her down into the tall grass, and during the rape she had cried and struggled. The smell of the crushed grass around her head was very strong, and this smell had become impressed upon her mind as part of the terrifying experience of being raped. It was still triggering her body to "cry" when she smelled crushed or fresh-mown grass. This was not a death experience; Alissa lived to a ripe old age in that lifetime, and she was not allergic to grass. It was not until her next life that the allergy was triggered.

Jean and Karen both had allergies to smoke, and both traced them to past lives. Jean went back to a past life in the 1400s in Ireland. A poor woman with several children and an incompetent husband, she lived in a small house that was in serious disrepair; she reported cooking with some fuel that was "in chunks, black and oily." (Although Jean had no name for this fuel, it was probably peat. Jean later said she had never heard of peat, but it was used for fires in some parts of Ireland for centuries.) The fuel produced a thick black oily smoke that was trapped in the house because the "opening" was faulty and blocked. Because of her cooking, she could not leave but had to stand at the stove and inhale this smoke. It made her cough, her eyes fill, and her throat hurt. In the end it probably killed her; she died in her thirties of a "lung problem," as her mother had before her.

Karen's smoke-related past life was entirely different. In addition to her allergy to smoke, Karen was also allergic to certain chemical smells; just which ones she could not identify. Karen went back to a life in the ninth century, probably in Greece or somewhere else around the Mediterranean. Karen lived in a small farming village at the foot of a volcano, and one day the volcano erupted. Karen and the other women tried to run from the ash, smoke, and smothering heat, but they also tried to save their children and could not move very fast. Karen and her children were overtaken by the deadly, chemical-laden smoke and ash, and died.

For both Karen and Jean, the smell of smoke (and some chemicals, in Karen's case) triggered all those old unconscious memories and their bodies reacted as if the old events were happening again.

Asthma is also sometimes related to past lives. Charles went back to his most recent past life, in which he had been trapped in a burning building and had inhaled smoke and could not breathe. He had been saved and survived, but had suffered lung damage that never completely left him. Now in this lifetime, the smell of smoke triggered asthma attacks.

There are some conditions in which people may think they have found the *cause* of the condition but have really not. This is particularly true of allergies, and asthma when it is triggered by an allergic reaction to something, like Charles's asthma, which was triggered by smoke. Charles was really allergic to smoke, but his reaction took the form of asthma rather than the usual running eyes and stuffed sinuses. Recurrent headaches may also be another case in point.

Many people with allergies have had tests that show that they are allergic to this or that substance: smoke, grass, dust, pollen, and so forth. They may then think that they have found the cause of their allergy. But they have not. What those tests really do is establish that your body reacts to those particular substances in certain unpleasant ways. But just why your body should do that is not revealed in the tests. All of the allergic clients I discussed above had had tests that demonstrated what they were allergic to, but those tests had not touched upon the basic causes. So although you may have had tests that show you what you are allergic to, the question of *why* that should be may only be answerable by examining your past lives. And as in Charles's case, this sometimes also seems to be true for people with asthma.

The thing to keep in mind here is that even some doctors overlook the fact that their tests for allergies do not tell us why their patient's body should react in the allergic way it does. In other words, some medical tests do not look for causes, but rather define symptoms. In our medically minded world, we are all apt to overlook this fact and think that the cause has been found. But to find after testing that a person has an allergy to grass may be simply stating the obvious, and may be what the patient already knew, too. But the reason they are allergic in the first place is what is sometimes found in past-life experience, and that can sometimes eliminate the allergy itself.

In the case of recurrent headaches, after medical tests a doctor may be able to categorize your headaches as migraines, tension headaches, or cluster headaches. With the rare tumor-caused headaches, tests can indeed accurately identify the reason: the tumor. But for the more usual kinds of recurrent headaches, the reason you have those headaches at all is not usually addressed. Why do your muscles tighten up in certain situations? Why do certain foods give you headaches? And why do migraines seem to spring upon you with no warning or reason?

So even after medical tests have given you some seeming explanation or categorization, as tests for allergies or headaches do, ask your doctor *why* your body reacts in these ways. Doctors are not usually asked this, and some doctors may not like it, but if they have no satisfactory answer, you may be dealing with a physical problem that got its start in a past-life experience.

A good many mysterious but seemingly physical problems can turn out to have past-life roots. Isabel had suffered from a lack of bladder control all her life. She had frequent attacks of cystitis as well, and suffered from painful intercourse. Doctors could not find any physical reason for these problems; they were, she was told by one, "all in her head." Isabel had heard that past lives can sometimes relieve physical problems, and she wanted to try. She went back to a recent lifetime in which she had been raped at ten by several soldiers. The pain was terrible and she was badly torn; she had almost died from loss of blood. She did not die, but she lost control of her sphincter muscles after this experience, and she had never been able to have a sexual relationship in that life. After she examined this past lifetime, Isabel's problems disappeared as if by magic.

Bert also suffered from a mysterious physical problem that had no apparent physical cause. He could not raise his left arm above his shoulder without intense pain and also had occasional pain in his right shoulder. There was nothing wrong with his arms or shoulders, the doctors said; for Bert too, his problem was "all in his head." And sure enough, like Isabel's, it was: Bert went back to a lifetime in which he had been hung by his arms as a punishment and tortured. Left alone without food or water, he had died hanging there, in intense pain. After recalling this experience, Bert's trouble, like Isabel's, vanished. I saw him a month later and he raised his arms high over his head in a victory grip and laughed.

Another client, Alex, had a similar problem: sharp pain in his right shoulder when he raised his arm above shoulder height. But the cause was different than in Bert's case. Alex went back into a past life in which his village had been attacked at night. While he was reaching up along the wall for his weapon, the attackers had speared him through the back just below his right shoulder, pinning him to the wall, where he died in great pain. For Alex, too, his pain was eliminated after he experienced this regression.

Sometimes a physical problem that is considered genetic or congenital is found to be related to a past life. An intriguing example is birthmarks. Birthmarks are usually considered to be caused by some defect in the genetic code or some damage that incurred in utero. Yet Dr. Ian Stevenson, who has investigated over 2,000 children who claim to consciously remember their most recent past lives, has found that many of them have birthmarks that are directly related to some past-life experience, usually a traumatic death experience.

One child that Stevenson investigated had birthmarks circling both wrists, and he consciously remembered dying as a man in his most recent past life. Thieves, whom he surprised while they were robbing his house, had bound his wrists behind his back with tight wire. After stealing what they could find, they had left him like that to die, and he had died there, in great pain from the tight wires that bound his wrists. The boy's birthmarks mirrored the terrible injuries caused by the wires. Dr. Stevenson has found numerous cases like this. In his book *Reincarnation and Biology: A Contribution to the Etiology of Birthmarks and Birth Defects,* he discusses his research into these cases.

Some of my own clients have had birthmarks that mirrored injuries sustained in a past life. In Chapter 4 I discussed Betty, the woman with the phobia for caterpillars, who had a birthmark on her back in the place where a burning caterpillar tent fell in her most recent past life. Another client, Mel, a man who reported a past life in which he had died after a painful snakebite, had two small birthmarks on his calf where the snake had bitten him. After his session, Mel volunteered the information that he had these birthmarks and showed them to me. I do not usually ask clients about birthmarks, and no client comes for past-life therapy for them, but it is possible that a good many people carry birthmarks that are related to past-life experience.

It would be wonderful to be able to say that after Betty and Mel examined their past lives, their birthmarks faded away. However, so far as I know, they didn't. Becoming aware of the past life cause of a birthmark does not seem to be a cure for it.

As Stevenson says, these birthmarks raise some fascinating questions. Exactly how does the mind or soul remember such an experience and stamp the new body, the fetus's body, with these scars of the old injury? And why? This is an area that badly needs research; beyond that, I cannot say. But these past-life-related birthmarks completely contradict the currently held beliefs about birthmarks. They may show us the power of mind (or soul) over body in its most dramatic form.

As I said above, both Isabel and Bert had been told that their problems were "all in their head." As it turns out, this statement is correct, in a way. At least it is correct if we suppose that the mind/soul in located in the head. As I hope this chapter indicates, our mind/soul apparently carries memories of severe physical trauma from one life into our next one, and these old traumatic experiences recreate the symptoms of the past-life experience in our new life, often mysterious symptoms that have no discernible medical cause. Just how it does this is completely unknown at the present time.

For several decades, medical science has acknowledged that some of our physical problems are "psychosomatic": that is, they are caused by some psychological factor. This psychological factor is, today, often considered to be "stress." The idea is that if we don't handle stress well, our bodies will react by getting sick. This is very possible and probably true. As we all know from personal experience, any physical problem, even the common cold, may worsen if we are rushed, worried, overworked, or trying to deal with too much all at once. The way we handle stress is certainly a big factor in our health.

But there seems to be another way that physical and health problems are "all in our heads": sometimes we seem to bring them with us as excess baggage from our past lives. Some can be dumped after the relevant past life is examined, as in most of the cases above; but sometimes they are perhaps not dumpable, as seems to be true of birthmarks.

The connections between mind and body are still uncertain, although they are being seriously investigated today by a good many physicians and researchers. But we see the results of this connection in the past-life causes of a wide assortment of physical problems. We can and often do bring physical problems with us into this life from our past lives, and when we do, we have the ability to dump this excess baggage in the past and free ourselves from the problems.

A word of warning, in closing. If you have a serious illness, or think you may have, you should see your doctor and take his advice. If you then want to augment his treatment by looking for any past lives that might be relevant, that's probably fine, no harm done, and you might find out that a past-life connection, if not an actual cause, is lurking there. If so, examining the past-life connection may help you deal better with the illness and may even speed up the treatment. But most really serious illnesses seem not to be caused entirely by past lives, and to seek past-life therapy first for them would merely postpone the medical treatment that you should be getting. In fact, most ethical past-life therapists will not accept a client for a serious medical problem unless he or she is under a doctor's care. They know it is a human tendency to want a quick, magical cure and to look for that first, postponing medical care as the last resort. But for the serious medical conditions, modern medical treatments are probably the quickest cure available and many times the only one.

But if you have been told that your "medical" problem is "all in your head," and if careful physical examinations show nothing that might be causing it, you may be dealing with a physical problem that has been dragged along from a past life, and probably unnecessarily.

CHAPTER TEN

VISIONS, DÉJÀ VU, NIGHTMARES, DREAMS

A good many people have mysterious dreams, nightmares, déjà vu experiences, or waking visions that turn out to be related to experiences in their past lives. This is especially true of recurrent dreams or nightmares, those that occur over and over, and this is true for children as well as for adults. I discuss children's experiences in Chapter 10; here I discuss adults' experiences. I will start with an experience very familiar to most people, the déjà vu experience. Some, but not all, of these can come from a past life, and a déjà vu experience that comes from a past life can be startling. It can also be either friendly or frightening.

There are several kinds of experiences called déjà vu; the phrase means "already seen." One common kind of déjà vu is brief and fleeting. It happens when you know exactly what a given person is about to say and then he says it, or when you walk into a room and have the immediate feeling that you have done this before. These fleeting experiences make people think they must be psychic, but the likelier explanation is that there is a sort of "lag" in their brain between what happens and their own perception of it. This is perfectly normal and happens to most people once in a while, and to some people more than others. It is not apt to be connected to past-life experience or psychic ability either.

However, experience with clients suggests that there may sometimes be another explanation for these fleeting déjà vu experiences. I once had a client, Rose, who had these experiences fairly

141

often, and who also had what are called "precognitive dreams." Precognitive dreams are dreams that later come true, sometimes in a tragedy, such as a death or a terrible accident, but not always.

The first thing to know about precognitive dreams is that the dream does not cause the event that later happens, tragic or not. A lot of people feel guilty about these dreams, so if you are one of those people, I assure you that you are not causing cars to crash or airplanes to nosedive by your dreams. Precognitive dreams seem to be more like warnings, and there are cases reported where the person who had such a dream was able to prevent the dreamed-of tragedy from happening by quick action, such as warning another person. So they do not always predict some coming tragedy that is inevitable. Or there may truly be nothing that can be done, and the warning is just to let you know that something is about to happen. But either way, the dreamer does not cause the event by dreaming about it. Some people have these precognitive dreams frequently; some never have a single one. You can usually spot people who have never had one: Look for the people who don't believe in them.

Rose had had precognitive dreams throughout her life, although they were of trivial, daily events, not tragedies to come. She also experienced the fleeting kind of déjà vu frequently. But Rose's experience was a bit different from the ordinary déjà vu experience. Rose said that sometimes when she had a déjà vu experience, such as being in a group and knowing what the next person to speak would say, or feeling as if she had been there before, she remembered that she had dreamed it a night or two before. Although she often remembered her precognitive dreams from the moment she awoke, sometimes she did not remember the dream until the event actually happened, and then the dream instantly came back to her memory.

This suggests the possibility that people who have this kind of fleeting déjà vu experience may have had a precognitive dream of the event, like Rose, but perhaps they just do not remember the dream. But when the dream comes true in a minor déjà vu experience in the next day or so, they still do not remember the dream, and here they are unlike Rose, who does remember the dream at that moment. So it seems strange and mysterious to them. Precognitive dreams themselves are strange and mysterious, but they may be the reason for this kind of déjà vu. Or the more conventional explanation for déjà vu may be the right one, that it is a kind of "lag" in our brains between what happens and our perception of it. Or both may be true, depending upon the given case. These fleeting déjà vu experiences are fascinating, but whatever their cause, this common kind of déjà vu seems to have nothing to do with past lives.

But another kind of déjà vu sometimes does. This is a rare occurrence, which may happen only once in a lifetime, and for most people, it probably never happens. General George Patton had a strong déjà vu experience of this kind when he was in France during World War II. He was standing on a slight rise looking down at the little valley beneath, and he suddenly "knew" that he had stood there long ago as an officer in the Roman Legion. It was as if he became that long-ago officer again, and he had a sudden powerful vision of that long-gone evening. He "saw" his men in their camp in the valley, preparing their suppers over their fires; he smelled the meat cooking, heard the men's casual talk and laughter, the sounds of the horses. It was a powerful vision that lasted for several minutes, and Patton believed that he had really been that long-ago Roman officer.

He had a similar experience in North Africa, and he became convinced that he had lived other lives as a military man. Although he never explored any of these past lives through hypnosis, he may well have been correct. If anyone seemed to be an old experienced soldier, it was certainly General Patton! One can easily believe that he had collected his military skills over centuries.

General Patton's experience was unusually clear and vivid. But many people have a somewhat similar experience. One of my clients, Alice, had a déjà vu experience of this type. When she was fourteen, Alice and her mother visited Europe. Alice had not wanted to go on the trip, preferring to spend the summer at home with her friends. She had found most of the trip boring; in the fourteen-year-old girl's estimation, it was "just a lot of old churches and museums." But one of their many stops was Amsterdam, and that was different.

Alice had loved Amsterdam. As they visited the old sections of town, Alice felt that she had been there before, had actually lived there. She felt as if she could stay there forever and be completely at home. She knew her way around the maze of old streets despite the changes; she recognized that some buildings were new but also recognized old ones and the changes that had been made to them. In Amsterdam, it was the young Alice who guided her mother through the old streets, and who usually knew what was around the next corner.

Ever since that experience in her teens, Alice had wondered if she might have lived before, in Amsterdam, and when she was in her thirties, she went back in hypnosis to that very life. She had lived there in the 1800s, or rather, had grown up there as Clara, the happy daughter of a loving widowed mother. They were poor, and her mother earned their living by doing housework for wealthier families, as she herself had begun to do in her teens. But when Clara was eighteen, she fell in love with a young man and soon was pregnant by him. Knowing how disappointed and angry her mother would be at this news, she ran away to another town and never returned to Amsterdam. But that long-ago Clara never lost her love for Amsterdam, and it was reawakened in Alice when she visited there at fourteen.

Many clients have had these déjà vu experiences about places where they have lived in past lives. It may not always be a place, such as a city; sometimes a client has an experience like this when seeing a particular house, or a style of house, or even a picture of a place, or a simple street scene. There is an immediate sense of familiarity, of knowing what's around the corner, what's inside. It may be something slight, seemingly unimportant. One of my clients had always loved white picket fences, although in this life she had never lived in a house that had one. She went back to a happy past life in which she had lived in a house with such a fence, and to her in that life, the fence had marked the boundary of her contented family life.

Even without strong déjà vu experiences, most people feel more interest in certain periods of history and certain places than in others. Many people in my workshops come because they have always loved a particular place and they feel drawn to it. It may be an old ruin they saw a picture of, or a landscape that they know they would feel at home in, or a city they feel they know. Or they may wonder why they have always had such an interest in the Italian Renaissance and love those clothes so much, or why they have such a yen for the sea, or enjoy Gregorian chants so much. Many of these interests turn out to be associated with past lives that the person has lived, often with happy past-life experiences.

Sometimes these hunches and interests take the form of dreams, or nightmares, or flashback experiences. My client Nat, who came for another problem entirely, said after the past-life session related to his problem that he had seen one of those same streets in a sort of waking vision he had experienced all his life. When he first awoke in the mornings, he would "see" a certain street scene, complete with the surrounding buildings; this would vanish instantly as he awoke more fully. In the past life we had just explored, Nat's most recent life, the street was in the old French Quarter of New Orleans and he had died there, in that street. Its buildings were the last things he saw before he left his body.

Nat had never been to New Orleans, but he made a trip there on his next vacation and found himself wandering bemused and delighted through a very familiar French Quarter. He noticed the changes and recognized some of the buildings, many of which have been kept pretty much the same over the decades. Nat lost something from this past-life regression, however: he no longer has his old waking vision of that New Orleans street.

These flashback experiences are not always so benign. I will discuss Barbara's case in more detail. Barbara had always felt sad and depressed and had a sense of guilt whenever the Civil War was mentioned. Even as a child, she had hated studying about it in school. When she was ten, her family had gone to visit Gettysburg, although she herself was almost afraid to go. The mere name "Gettysburg" depressed her. When they arrived at the battlefield, she had suddenly felt an overwhelming sadness and burst into sobs; she had been unable to get out of the car. Strange behavior for a girl of ten.

More than twenty-five years later, when Barbara was in her thirties, she came to see me, and it was an emergency visit. She was in trouble, and a friend had suggested that hypnosis might help her. She did not come for past-life work as such, and it later developed that she believed reincarnation was impossible.

Barbara's real trouble had begun when her teenaged son had begun to watch the PBS TV miniseries by Ken Burns, *The Civil War*, as a class assignment. Barbara knew she did not want to watch it but she also felt she should do more to challenge her irrational feelings about the Civil War, and decided that watching this program would help her do that. So, with some trepidation, she settled down on the couch to watch the first installment with her two children.

As all who have seen this documentary know, this is a very moving and powerful treatment of the Civil War, incorporating old photographs, letters, and the music of the time. It was too much for Barbara. Five minutes after it began, she was upstairs sobbing on her bed, and it was a full half hour before she could get her feelings under control, despite her anxious husband's help and reassurances.

Barbara told me that the next ten days were like a nightmare. She had felt "like a zombie," walking around "in a daze" and doing her chores with no real connection to anything or anyone. She was depressed and felt "something like grief, or guilt," and frequently found tears just running down her face. Indeed, they ran down her cheeks as she sat in my office. She apologized for her "silly tears" as she wiped at her face. This had been going on for almost two weeks now, and she hoped that through hypnosis I could give her suggestions that she no longer felt this way.

To me, it sounded like a past-life experience surfacing, but I did not know that and I did not tell Barbara I thought it might be. Instead, when she was in hypnosis, I asked her Upper Mind to take us where we needed to go, and sure enough, it took us to a past-life experience.

Barbara went back to a life as Sarah, a woman living in Virginia, born in the early 1800s. Barbara entered the past-life memory at a time about ten years before the Civil War (or "The War Between the States," as Sarah called it later in the session). At that time, Sarah and her husband were living happily with their unmarried teenaged daughter. They had a married son, Richard, who lived nearby in his own home with his wife.

Ten years later, by the time of the war years, Sarah's daughter was married and her son Richard's wife had died in childbirth. Both Richard and the daughter's husband had joined the Confederate Army. During the war Sarah's household consisted of herself and her husband, their daughter and her two young sons, and Richard's young daughter. A crowded household, and given the conditions of the war years Sarah described, life was not easy for them.

Sarah's son Richard died at Gettysburg. This was a terrible grief for Sarah, but she said her husband took it harder than she did: he was not well, and after Richard's death, Sarah said, he "just gave up." She herself had dreaded and half expected Richard's death all along, for as she said, there was "so much death, death was everywhere, every family lost people."

Sarah continued with her busy life, raising Richard's daughter and helping her daughter raise her two sons. The daughter's husband came home wounded from the war, and although he recovered, he was never able to do much heavy work on the farm. After the war, life continued to be hard; they had little and struggled to keep what they did have. Her husband died before her. She herself died in her late sixties of an illness, living with her daughter and still busy with her grandchildren's lives.

Although Sarah apparently accepted her son Richard's death, she never really grieved for him: in a way, she was just too busy. But she was also "putting it off" in a peculiar way. For years after the war she hoped to be able to go to Gettysburg to try to find his grave and bring his body back for "proper" burial in the family plot. Then she could truly grieve for him. She had been told that he had been buried "in the field," but she believed she could find his grave and bring him back home. Many families did this, she said, helped by survivors' memories and crude markers that had been raised to mark the graves. However, because of her husband's and son-in-law's poor health, and also because they had no money to spare, they were never able to do this.

Sarah died feeling sad and bitter that Richard was still buried "up north among the Yankees," away from home and family. She felt guilty that she had not done her duty to him. These feelings, rather than grief for Richard's death itself, had been carried forward into Barbara's life and were said to be the cause of her sadness and guilt. Although to some extent these feelings had been present all her life, they had been brought violently into awareness by the segment of the Civil War series she had seen. It was as if she still felt at a deep level that she had unfinished business to do.

After the death experience had been briefly explored, I asked Barbara (as Barbara) if she could leave all that sadness and guilt "back there," and she said she could. I suggested that she "go back" and thank Sarah for her courage and for all her other good qualities, which she did, and we left the Sarah life "in the past."

Barbara called a week or so later to tell me that her symptoms had lifted and that she was "back to normal." Furthermore, thoughts of the Civil War no longer elicited even her old, lifelong feelings of sadness. She had watched the next installment of the Civil War documentary, and although she had felt sadness, it was "a normal sadness," as she put it.

A few months later Barbara called again to tell me that she, her husband, and their children had taken a week's vacation and driven down to Washington, D.C. Barbara had insisted that they include Gettysburg in the trip as well.

She had felt none of the old depression when she was there. She had, on impulse, purchased some red roses, Sarah's favorite flower, taken them to the battlefield, and left them at a marker commemorating those who had died there. She had experienced "a kind of nostalgia" when she did this, but that was all; she laughed wryly when she said she had done this "for Sarah, whoever she was, because she never could put flowers on her son's grave." Barbara was still not sure whether Sarah had really lived or was a figment of her own imagination, but she had decided that it didn't really matter. After more than five years, Barbara's symptoms have not returned.

Barbara's flashback experience seems to have been lurking all her life, in the form of her lifelong sadness about the topic of the Civil War, but it was violently triggered by the Civil War documentary. This may happen more than we realize. I have known other clients who reacted in unexpected ways to movies and whose reactions were coming from events in a past life. Anytime a person has a sudden strong and unexplainable reaction to a film or even a picture of a place, there may be a past-life involved.

Sometimes past-life experiences present themselves in the form of recurrent nightmares, and these can be truly terrifying. Michelle was such a client, and she was the very first past-life client I worked with.

Michelle had experienced a recurrent nightmare from infancy. In her earliest months she had frequently awakened screaming, much to her parents' fright. As the years went by, she began to speak of "the man" after these nightmares, which occurred several times a week. All this so alarmed her parents that they had taken her to a child psychiatrist for treatment. As she grew up, she went to other therapists, but they all found her a normal little girl and said that the nightmares would disappear as she got older.

Many children's nightmares do disappear as the child gets older, so that was a reasonable thing to assume. However, Michelle's nightmares did not disappear. They became less frequent, and by the time she reached her thirties, they were occurring only two or three times a month. However, Michelle had gradually noticed an ominous change in them, and it frightened her.

In the nightmare, Michelle suddenly awoke and opened her eyes, or thought she did, and found the room filled with a silvery-blue light, something like moonlight. Standing in this light was "an old man," dressed in "old-fashioned" baggy clothes and wearing a wide-brimmed hat. She could not see his eyes clearly, but she knew he stared out at her from under his hat brim, and she also knew he hated her. Michelle would scream with fear at this point and both the man and the strange light would fade away. But Michelle was left cold and shaking and too frightened to go back to sleep.

As Michelle remembered this nightmare from her childhood, the man had stood across the room from her bed, but over the years he had slowly come closer until now, when she was in her thirties, he stood very close to her bed. Michelle felt that he had come to get her, and that when he finally reached the bedside, he would reach out and touch her and she would die. This was, of course, a terrifying idea, and she had become afraid to go to sleep.

Michelle, like Barbara, came for a session because a friend had suggested that hypnosis, which she had never before tried, might help her be free of the nightmare. She was so frightened of the nightmare that her whole body shook as she told me about it. I did not consider the possibility of past-life involvement. As I said, Michelle was my first past-life client, and I was not thinking in those terms.

One thing that had occurred to me, of course, was that there was a childhood abuse experience behind the nightmare. I raised this question very cautiously with Michelle, but she only laughed and said that her other therapists had thought that too, but that there was no evidence to support the idea. Anyway, as she pointed out, her parents believed that the nightmare had begun in the first weeks of her life, making an abuse experience very unlikely. Michelle added that even if that was the answer, she wanted to know it.

When she was in hypnosis, I first tried some conventional hypnosis techniques that are believed to be effective with nightmares; however, Michelle herself, in hypnosis, told me that "the man was still there." At that point, I asked her to go back to a time shortly before she last saw the man, if she had ever seen him. I was still expecting to find some old childhood abuse situation, and wanted to approach it cautiously. However, Michelle began to speak of something entirely different. After a long pause, she said:

M: I'm sitting on a hillside—I'm wearing a long dress, old-fashioned—

T: Sitting on a hill? Are you a child?

M: No—I'm a woman. There's a child—

T: A child? Is that you?

M: No—I'm the woman. I'm her mother. She's gathering flowers—

T: Michelle, where are you?

There was a long pause. Then she said:

M: I think I'm in Spain. But I've never been to Spain—

At that point, I realized that she had slipped spontaneously into a past life. I also realized that I had never worked with past-life regressions and wasn't sure how to proceed, so I told her to "close the door on all that" and come back to the present time in my office. I then roused her from hypnosis. When she sat up, she was bewildered.

"What was that all about?" she asked.

I told her I was not sure but that anyway our time was up, as indeed it was, so we should wait to explore it in our next session, two weeks hence. I spent those two weeks trying to find out everything I could about past-life regression. This was in the mid-1970s, and very little had been written about past-life therapy, but I did find one book, just published, that told me what I needed to know. When Michelle came for her next session, we proceeded, very cautiously, and this was her story.

That hillside in Spain was part of Michelle's death experience in that lifetime, as was the mysterious man of her nightmare. However, when we explored the life at that second session, we were able to put together the whole life in its proper order. Michelle had been Anne, a girl living in a seaport town in England in the 1800s. Anne's father had died when Anne was very young, and although she and her widowed mother were poor, they were not poverty-stricken and Anne had a frugal but pleasant life.

When she was fifteen, her mother became ill, and knowing she was dying, she made an arrangement for Anne to marry an old family friend, a prosperous shopkeeper of the town, William. William was in his forties, and wanted an heir to inherit his business. Anne was delighted at first. William was generous and wanted his wife to live well, so Anne had pretty new clothes, a nice house, and a carriage to ride around the town in. However, she did not become pregnant, and soon became bored with her "old" set-in-his-ways husband. The inevitable happened: she fell in love with a young Spanish sailor whose ship put in to the port. They ran away together to his village in Spain, where he introduced her as his wife.

They were happy, and Anne soon had a baby daughter. Although her lover was away on his ship for long periods of time, and the village women never quite accepted the "English woman," Anne learned the language and got along well enough. She was reasonably content raising her daughter.

Then one day, while her lover was away, Anne and her daughter, then about seven, were on a stony hillside near the village gathering flowers. The child brought them to Anne, who tried to weave them into a coronet for her. Then suddenly William appeared, striding up the hillside with the village women behind him. He had apparently tracked her down and had obviously told the women the true situation, for they began to yell at her and call her terrible names. One of them picked up one of the small stones that were scattered over the hillside and threw it at her, and the other women joined in, all screaming at her, calling her "witch" and "whore."

Anne died there, stoned to death. The last thing she saw was William standing over her body, looking down at her with scorn and hatred from under his wide hat brim.

He was the man of her nightmare. After we had examined this terrible experience, I asked Michelle to place herself, as Michelle, in a safe clearing in the woods and bring William there. Then I directed her to ask him what he had wanted all these years, although it seemed obvious. Sure enough, he said he wanted *her.* I then directed her to ask for his forgiveness for having run away, and to forgive him also, for having stood passively by and let the village women stone her to death. I also directed her to tell William that that life was over, and that she was living another life and that he must go and do the same. He agreed to all this, they parted amiably, and he went on his way.

Forgiveness scenes like this are often helpful in past-life therapy, but they may not be, strictly speaking, necessary. In any case, Michelle's nightmare went away and after more than twenty years she has still not had it again. I once asked her if she ever missed it. She laughed and said she did not, but she also said she sometimes wondered where William was these days, and doing what.

Psychology has no easy answer for déjà vu experiences like the ones above, or for visions, dreams, and nightmares like Michelle's that seem to have no cause. Most of our dreams and nightmares are probably not caused by past-life experiences. But there are certain differences between a vision, dream, or nightmare caused by a past-life experience and the more ordinary kinds.

For one thing, when these experiences are caused by past-life events, they seem real; they are usually very clear and strongly visual, and carry a strong emotional reaction with them. They often include people in old-fashioned clothes, as Michelle's frightening man wore, or take place in another century or a place that is foreign to you. They are usually recurrent, and they are always pretty much the same, as were Nat's vision of the New Orleans street scene and Michelle's nightmare of the man staring at her from under his hat brim. Another difference is that in these experiences, nothing magical happens. In an ordinary dream or nightmare, the scene shifts suddenly, illogically, from place to place. People may change into other people or even into animals, and you may even find yourself flying through the skies. These things do not happen in dreams or nightmares caused by past-life experiences.

There have been many theories of what causes dreams and nightmares, ranging from the "dream as symbol" theories of psychoanalysis to the "dream as random firing of neurons" theories of modern biomedical researchers. Although many people believe that psychology has "proven" dreams to be repressed wishes, this is really an old theory and few if any psychologists believe it today. Some dream researchers have found that dreams sometimes seem to help us solve problems we are facing in our daily lives (and this is one of Adler's theories, as I discussed in Chapter 2). In the case of recurrent dreams that occur for years, the theory is that we are trying to solve a long-standing problem. Another interesting idea is that dreams are a sort of filing system for the brain: at night we process the events of the day just passed and get them arranged in an orderly manner.

It is also recognized today that some dreams do come from actual experiences we have had. This is especially obvious in nightmares, where a person may relive a terrible experience over and over in the same nightmare, and such an experience can reappear as a flashback experience, too. The combat flashbacks sometimes suffered by war veterans are a tragic example, and people may also have recurrent dreams of an accident they experience.

This is basically what seems to happen with dreams, nightmares, and flashbacks stemming from past-life experience. In other words, some dreams, nightmares, and flashbacks come from real events, and those events may be in our present lives or our past lives. Such dreams, nightmares, and flashbacks are usually recurrent, and emotionally powerful. Recurrent visions, too, that happen while the person is awake, such as Nat's waking vision of the street scene or General Patton's vision, are a kind of flashback, and may come from real-life experiences as well as past-life ones.

"Ordinary" dreams or nightmares, whatever they may be, are different from the recurrent dreams and nightmares caused by past-life experiences. Sometimes it is easy to identify the cause: perhaps it was a movie you saw last night, or an argument you had with your boss, or a book you read just before you went to bed. If you went to bed with a problem on your mind, you would do well to pay attention to your dreams, because perhaps your unconscious mind is trying to show you a possible solution to the problem in the language of symbols it seems to favor in ordinary dreams. Even nightmares can come from these causes.

But if you have a recurrent dream or nightmare, or a recurrent flashback or vision like Nat's, and if it is visually vivid and clear, carries strong emotional freight, and has no magical happenings, and if you cannot explain it logically, you may be dealing with something that you have brought with you from a past life. If in addition, the dream or nightmare includes people in old-fashioned clothes, or involves living in an old house, or is set in a time before you were born, the chances are pretty good that your mind is reminding you of something that happened to you in a past life, perhaps trying to call your attention to some very old unfinished business.

CHAPTER ELEVEN

CHILDREN

Have you ever wondered what newborn babies are dreaming of? Most newborns sleep at least twenty-one hours of the day; the rest of the time they are eating or getting ready to sleep again. And anyone who has watched a sleeping baby knows that they often seem to be dreaming. Their eyes move from side to side, they make small movements and sounds, and sometimes they wake as if from a nightmare, screaming as if with terror. All of these behaviors indicate dreaming in older children and adults. But what do babies have to dream about? Could babies be dreaming of the past lives they have lived? Are they "filing" them in their new brains the way we would organize a new filing cabinet, getting ready to use all of those past experiences and past learning in the new life they have just entered? This is an exciting idea and one that may well be true.

Some children seem spontaneously to remember their past lives. Perhaps all children do but we simply don't recognize the clues they give us. After all, in our Western culture, if our two-year-old starts to talk about her other mommy, or the job he used to have, or complains that she never had to eat broccoli before when she was a grown-up, we are apt to assume our toddler has picked this up on TV or in some story. And children do fantasize, we know. So we are very likely to ignore these clues, and by the time the child is five or six, he or she has stopped talking this way.

But we may be doing our children a great injustice. Perhaps they are really telling us something about a past life, and we should pay more attention to their stories. Some people have paid attention, and what they have found is fascinating.

I have mentioned Dr. Ian Stevenson earlier in this book, and I will discuss his work in more detail here. Since the 1960s, Dr. Stevenson, a psychiatrist at the University of Virginia, has paid attention to these children's stories. Over decades of careful work, Stevenson has investigated children in numerous countries who spontaneously talk about their most recent past lives. Stevenson is especially interested in children who give enough information to make checking the facts of the recent life possible: names, places, events in the previous person's life, and similar details. Most children do not give this kind of detailed information, but Stevenson has investigated over 2,000 who did.

When the child gives enough details, Stevenson and his colleagues first go to the child's home and interview the child and his or her family and other relatives. Then they go to the place where the child reports having lived in the previous life to check the details the child gives against the actual details of the previous person's life. Sometimes they have been able to take the child back to the old town, and when they do, some of these children have been able to find their way around the town, lead the way to their old home, and recognize the various relatives from the previous life. They often comment on changes that have been made since their death in the previous life, although not all these comments are approving of the changes! They act the way we all act if we go back to a place we lived in once but have not been back to for many years, recognizing buildings, streets, old friends, noticing changes and commenting on them. As I discussed in Chapter 9, some of these children have birthmarks that reflect the way the previous person died; and some have phobias or other problems that are clearly related to the death or some other traumatic event in the previous life, too.

Stevenson's major interest has been in assessing whether or not these children's stories about their past lives could be true, and he has not used them for therapy. Nor does he use hypnosis with the children. Their statements about their prior lives are spontaneous and made rather casually when they are conscious and awake. But Stevenson's findings indicate connections between a good many problems, as well as other attributes, and the child's prior life. And in most cases, the details check out.

Stevenson's work has been criticized, unfairly I think, on the grounds that most of his cases stem from countries where reincarnation is supposedly taken for granted and where children would be encouraged to talk about their prior lives. This assumption is a sweeping generalization, and like most sweeping generalizations, it is greatly exaggerated. It may also be somewhat chauvinistic: it seems to be really based on a notion that only if the cases come from some European country or the United States, where belief in reincarnation is not common, can they be taken seriously.

In any case, although it is true that Stevenson does not include American cases in his early writings, he does include some in his book *Children Who Remember Past Lives,* published in 1987 by the University Press of Virginia. Furthermore, many of his cases, whether from Western or Eastern countries, come from areas where reincarnation is not taken for granted at all. Others come from areas where reincarnation may be taken for granted but where to remember your past life is considered the worst of bad omens for the future and no family would encourage a child to talk about a prior life. And many involve children in families that have no belief in reincarnation and, in some cases, an actual dislike of the idea.

Stevenson is not alone in all of this. Carol Bowman, a woman who originally had no particular interest in past lives, discovered almost by accident that her five-year-old son's intense fear of loud booming sounds came from a past life. The boy had also spontaneously told her that he was once a soldier. A visiting hypnotist friend became curious about this statement and the boy's fear of loud explosive sounds, and with Bowman's permission, he regressed him. He went back to a past life as a young soldier in the Civil War in which he had been severely wounded on a battlefield, with loud booming sounds all around him.

One interesting thing about Bowman's son's experience is that he had a recurrent patch of eczema on his wrist at the place where he was wounded in the Civil War. After he explored this past life, the eczema disappeared and it has not returned.

Bowman's eight-year-old daughter also had a severe fear, that the house would burn, and when the hypnotist friend regressed her, she went back to a past life in which she had burned to death in a house fire. All this intrigued Bowman, and when she later realized that her children's fears and her son's eczema were gone, she became seriously interested. When she encountered Stevenson's work, she began to wonder how many American children spoke of their past lives.

She advertised in a national magazine and made television appearances, asking for parents whose children talked of their past lives to get in touch with her. The response was overwhelming. Although most of the children did not report any checkable details, and Bowman herself has not checked the details when they did give them, many of the parents themselves had checked details when they could, and many of them turned out to be accurate. Bowman has published a book about these children's memories, *Children's Past Lives*, published by Bantam Books in 1997.

Both Stevenson and Bowman found that typically these children begin to mention their former lives when they are very young, often when they are barely able to talk. They make statements that compare their former lives with their present ones. Often these are complaints at the restrictions placed upon them now, apparently feeling that they are adults, not children, and should not be treated so rudely!

These children also often have problems that stem from their past lives, and these are similar to the problems adults bring in from their past lives and that we see in past-life therapy. But as a rule, children under five are difficult and sometimes impossible to hypnotize, so for them past-life therapy as it is usually practiced is impossible. But many have theorized that children spend most of their time in a trance state anyway, and Bowman has developed a method that makes use of this idea. She has found that even the youngest child can be helped simply and easily and in a way that any loving parent can do. Bowman gives directions for her method in her book. She stresses the importance of accepting whatever the child says without laughter or argument, and of reassuring the young child that he or she is in a new, loving home now, with a family that will be there for them.

After the age of five or six, children are more responsive to formal hypnosis; indeed, most children over six are very hypnotizable and enter altered states easily. They can rapidly access the trouble-some past life, examine the causes of the trouble, and leave it in the past at the direction of the therapist. Instructed to remain calm, comfortable, and interested, they do, and there is rarely any trauma from this approach. Reassuring suggestions are best for ending any past-life session with a child, and a parent should always be present to give security to the child and to back up these healing suggestions.

Although not many past-life therapists have worked with children in the past, this situation is changing and more and more are doing so. A pioneer in past-life therapy with children is Dr. Evelyn Fuqua. A child guidance specialist and school counselor for over thirty years, she discovered that children often have memories of past lives that cause them trouble in the present life. These memories may be clear and vivid or jumbled and confused with events in their present lives, and may appear as dreams or "fantasy" tales. They may also appear suddenly in response to severe stress in the child's life. In her article "Using Past-Life Concepts in Child Therapy," published in the *Journal of Regression Therapy*, Vol. IV, no. 1, Spring 1989, Fuqua says she has found that children accept the idea of reincarnation easily. It is, she says, as if reincarnation is "something that they have known but have forgotten."

For many children, a formal regression using hypnosis is not necessary. Fuqua recommends encouraging children to talk about the memories and to reassure them that they are safe now. This is certainly the first approach to take, and one I try first myself. But if this does not work, or for older children having nightmares or troublesome spontaneous memories, a true regression may be needed.

All kinds of problems may stem from past lives, and this is as true for children as for adults. And as also for adults, the value of therapy for children does not depend upon whether or not a child has previously consciously remembered a past life. Nor does it seem to injure the child in any way to examine a past life calmly and comfortably. In fact, children enjoy the experience, although for them it fades to insignificance afterward. They seem to realize, perhaps more clearly than adults sometimes do, that the past life is in the past and that their task is to get on with their present life— and without the problem that seemed so important before.

I recall Jamie, a boy of eight who had nightmares of being trapped in a burning building and who had great difficulty sitting still in school. In fact, his teachers had labeled him hyperactive. Jamie had never had any conscious memory of any past life, or at least his parents had not noticed any clues.

Jamie went rapidly into a light trance state and reported his most recent past life, early in this century, in which he had died in a burning one-room schoolhouse. A farm boy and very tired from farm chores, he had fallen asleep while sitting quietly in his corner seat. When he awoke, the room was full of smoke. A fire had started, probably from the wood stove used. He realized he was alone in the room and had been overlooked because of the thick smoke when the teacher shepherded the rest of the children out of the burning building. In this past life, Jamie had died in the fire, from smoke inhalation.

This past-life experience explained both of Jamie's problems, his nightmare of being trapped in a burning building and his troubles sitting still in school, and both disappeared after the session. It also explained his asthma, a condition Jamie had not come to therapy for but from which his mother said he had always suffered; this, too, vanished.

Mack was a nine-year-old with a severe phobia for water. Mack was even afraid to take baths, and in the shower he panicked if he got water on his face or head. Mack went back, as one might have guessed, to a life in which he had drowned; he had been a man sailing a small boat that had overturned. Mack, like Jamie, had had no apparent conscious memory of this past life, but after he retrieved it, his phobia disappeared. As always with children, I gave both Jamie and Mack hypnotic suggestions at the beginning of their regressions to remain calm and comfortable and interested throughout, and at the end of the regressions, to leave the past life and all the troubles in the past. They followed both of these instructions.

Many children have phobias and nightmares. Most of these troubles disappear by themselves as the child grows older and they are gone by the time he or she reaches adulthood. But some phobias and nightmares linger into adulthood, and these do not seem to go away by themselves at all. (I discuss adult phobias in Chapter 4 and nightmares in Chapter 10.) But it seems unnecessary and even cruel to let a child suffer from these problems all through childhood, hoping they will fade away by themselves. And of course, some do not fade away.

It is possible that most of these mysterious problems come from past lives, but that only those from the most recent life or those that have been developed from more than one past life linger into adulthood. It looks that way from the evidence now, but there has been no research on children's past lives that considers this question so it is hard to know. But a few quiet moments with a caring and receptive parent, as Bowman and Fuqua suggest, or a session or two of past-life therapy, might be able to quickly and easily get rid of all these fears and nightmares that are said to be so common among children.

In Chapter 10, I discussed Michelle's recurrent nightmare, a lifelong trouble that did not fade with adulthood and that had cost her a great deal of time and money for therapy, not to mention causing concern for her sanity. All her life, Michelle had secretly feared that there was something seriously wrong with her mind. This fear unquestionably affected her entire life. It certainly influenced her parents' view of her; they thought she was "crazy," and at the age of eight, they sent her to a child psychiatrist for therapy, which was unproductive. Her college roommate, and later her husband, shared their view of her "craziness"; she shared it herself. Past-life therapy did not exist when Michelle was a child, but today, it would be completely unnecessary for Michelle and those who loved her to suffer all this. It is very possible that her nightmare could have been easily eliminated early in her life, either by the gentle techniques recommended by Bowman and Fuqua in her very early years, or by past-life therapy using hypnotic regression when she was a bit older. She would not have had to wait until she was in her thirties to be free of the nightmare, and would not have had to live with the fear that she was "crazy" for all those years.

Children who consciously remember their past lives follow a certain pattern. Stevenson has found it in his researches and Bowman finds it in the stories parents send her. Typically, children begin to speak of the past life when they are around two or three years old, continue to speak of it for a few years, and then after they are five or six they gradually stop speaking of it. By the time they are ten, most have forgotten all about it and are well integrated into their present lives. But sometimes they still carry the scars from the past life—the fears or nightmares or other problems they brought in with them—and they may carry them all their lives. Stevenson found, as did Bowman, that these children are normal, well-functioning children, often very bright. This finding should reassure any parents who think there is something wrong with a child who starts to tell them all about how much better things were in his or her other life!

A pioneer in past-life research, psychologist Dr. Helen Wambach, tells in her book *Reliving Past Lives: The Evidence Under Hypnosis,* published in 1978 by Harper & Row, of a five-year-old who was brought to her for therapy long before past-life therapy even existed. This little boy, whom Wambach calls "Peter," was hyperactive, rushing from toy to toy in Wambach's office, unable to settle down. The one thing he could be still for was sitting with Wambach and talking about his life as a policeman. Peter said he liked basketball and was a smoker, and he didn't understand why he could not smoke now. Peter also said that as a policeman he had been assigned to traffic control, and his frightened parents told Wambach that one day Peter had been found standing in the street directing traffic; that was why they had brought him for therapy. Although Wambach was was able to help him some, she says that a better understanding of what Peter was trying to tell her would have helped him more. Perhaps he was describing his past life to her.

Along with problems, people bring talents and interests into this life from their past lives, and these will usually be present in childhood. Children need to be encouraged by parents to express their natural talents, to pursue their natural interests. These may be very different from anyone else's in the family. The child with a talent for art or an interest in World War I aircraft may be the only one in the family with these attributes, but they are legitimate for the child and may well be related to one of his or her past lives, perhaps the most recent one, perhaps a life farther back in time.

The most obvious example of this is found with child prodigies, of course, and they seem to demand that their talent, which is so strong that we call it genius, be recognized and encouraged. They act as if they know exactly what they are here for this time and they set about it with no hesitation and no tolerance for anyone who tries to stop them. But the more ordinary child may have a lesser talent and be less sure of it, and children in a family where that talent is discouraged or ridiculed may well slide away from expressing it, and have the lifelong feeling that something important is missing without quite knowing what. And they are right: something important is missing.

I have worked with many adult clients who discovered quite unexpectedly that they came into this lifetime with the goal of pursuing some particular talent or interest as a career, and they had demonstrated and enjoyed that talent in childhood. But their families had in some way discouraged them from pursuing it, or circumstances had prevented it, and they had chosen some other path.

Claire was such a client. A suburban housewife with a happy family, she came to me because of a phobia and feelings of general discontent with her life. When she went to the moment of planning her birth into this lifetime, and I asked her what her goal was this time, she suddenly realized that she had intended to pursue her talent for music, but she had not done so. She had been raised in a family that believed that women should focus their energy on building a home and family, and the pressure of this belief had dissuaded Claire from her serious interest and talent in music.

This sort of thing happens not just to women. It happened to Ron, who came for therapy in his forties for anxiety attacks he was having in his car on the way to work. In pursuing the reason for the anxiety attacks, Ron went back to his childhood love for astronomy, begun in a past life. In the time of choosing to be born into this present lifetime, he realized he had set a life's goal to pursue astronomy as a career this time. His family, however, believed that being an accountant was the best thing for him; his father and two uncles were accountants and Ron would be able to enter the family firm. He did: a dutiful son, he became an accountant in the family firm, as planned. Now in his forties, Ron's body itself was telling him, through the anxiety attacks on the way to work, that being an accountant was not right for him, or at least, not enough. Both Claire and Ron took back their talents and interests as hobbies, once they realized they were legitimate for them. Ron also enrolled in an introductory course in astronomy in the local college, and his anxiety attacks stopped.

It is important for parents to recognize that their children have lived before. We are privileged to be their parents. They honor and grace us by choosing us; they trust us to create for them the right environment for them to grow in. But they are not blank slates created by genes alone. They do not belong to us, and we cannot "mold" them to our liking without great cost to them. They are visitors, passing through our care, ready to do their share to create a good friendship with us, to love us even, if we are truly ready to do those things with them, person to person. They may be working out some old relationship problem with us, and we can best help them do that by recognizing their individuality and their ultimate right to shape their own lives. Or perhaps they may have simply wanted to continue a good relationship with us from the past, or they may have no past-life connections with us and chose us because we looked as if we would be good parents for them.

But whatever their reasons for choosing us, they are unique people who come equipped with past histories that influence them both negatively and positively. They need our help to get rid of the negatives that they may have brought in from their past lives, and to help them develop the strengths and positive attributes they have also brought with them.

As parents, it may also be important to us that we understand whatever past-life relationships we may have had with our children, and what other past-life experiences we have had that shape our attitudes toward our children or toward being parents at all. Julie, whom I discussed in Chapter 7, was actually afraid of her domineering young son because of two past-life situations with domineering men in which, as it turned out, her son was not even involved! Yet those past-life situations had shaped the ways in which she had raised her son to a profound degree. Had Julie known her own past-life history, she might have accepted her son more easily and lovingly and been less afraid to set the rules and insist upon them. In many ways, the manner in which we accept and deal with parenthood may be at least partly shaped by our own past-life experiences, both good and bad. Knowing those experiences can help us become the good parents we want to be and to accept our children as individuals and friends, and to love them freely and openly as the precious visitors they are.

As I said above, past-life therapy with children, as a field, has just begun. The earliest workers with past-life regressions believed that even for adults, accessing past lives could be dangerous, and that it was definitely not something to do with children. In those years, in fact, the hypnotic suggestion was usually given to all clients that the person would have no memory of their regression afterward. This caution was probably wise, since so little was known about regressions at that time.

Gradually we have learned that far from being dangerous, past-life regressions are helpful to people, and most helpful if they remember the session. We also know now that properly handled, regressions are something from which children can also benefit and actually enjoy. I say "properly handled" because, like Bowman and Fuqua, I believe that for adults and children alike, regressions should always be done calmly and comfortably, and never with highly emotional reliving of traumatic situations: this approach is indeed very stressful and upsetting. But under the right conditions, we know that children can often be helped with past-life regression, and often, even more easily than adults. Children seem very ready to remember their past lives, but then to leave them in the past and get on with their new, present lives.

CHAPTER TWELVE

———

THE INTERLIFE

For most past-life therapists, exploring the interlife, the time between lives, is always a part of past-life therapy as well as group workshop regressions. Most therapists try to access the interlife after the client's most recent life so clients can discover the choices they made and the goals they set for themselves before being born into their present life. In this chapter I discuss various interlife experiences and the kinds of choices people make before they come into their present lives. I include four taped transcript excerpts for illustration.

There are different experiences people have during the interlife. Some seem to go through the familiar and well-publicized Near-Death Experience (NDE), but others do not. Many people today have heard of the NDE, but I will describe it briefly for those who have not.

The NDE experience has happened to thousands of people during illness or surgery, or during or after an accident. The person is very near death, and has sometimes been declared clinically dead. People say they leave their body and float above it; they see the medical or ambulance staff down below, working over their body, trying to resuscitate them. Then they hear a rushing sound and feel themselves drawn rapidly through a tunnel or some other dark place toward an intense bright light that gets stronger as they approach it. They feel warm and comfortable as they move toward the light, and have feelings of bliss and joy. They see figures waiting for them in the light, people they have loved and who have died, and sometimes a religious figure. At this point they hear a voice that tells them that their time is not yet: they must go back and finish their work in life. They feel sad and even angry about this, but suddenly find themselves dropped back into their body.

People coming back from an NDE are not always happy to be back. Being back means pain, and a slow recovery from the injury or illness, and picking up the old daily chores again. But most of them also have a new sense of mission, and a new and lasting sense of calmness about life and their place in it. Many become more involved with spiritual concerns and feel that they have become better people because of the NDE. It is a profound experience, and those who have had it never forget it and never seem to lose the effects of those few moments while they were "dead."

Some people report this experience after a death in a past-life regression. But when you look at the transcripts of these cases, you can often see that the therapist has led the person into it by "suggesting" the bright light, the tunnel, the waiting figures, and all the rest. These suggestions from the therapist will sometimes produce an experience like the NDE, but without such direct instructions, most people do not report it, although they do talk about diffused bright light around them.

If people are simply told to "go rapidly through your death and to the moment right after you have died," most people say they float more or less gently out of their body at death, float above it and realize that they have died. If they are then instructed to "move on to the next thing that happens," they say they float away into a place of diffused brightness; sometimes it is a little foggy. This is not usually the focused, powerful light of the NDE, but instead a comfortable diffused brightness, a bright mist that surrounds them.

Some people continue to float peacefully until they realize that there are other people around. They describe these people as their "group" or "friends," and say that they are people they have known in various other lives, including the life they just left. They spend some time with these people, although they cannot say how much time, and finally make the decision to return, to be born again. They decide on what goals they will attempt to reach this time, and choose other elements of their new birth. In the taped transcripts below, Betty's is typical of this kind of interlife experience.

Others do not say they meet any group or any other people at all. Instead, they float peacefully in a warm, pleasant, bright place until they suddenly realize that it is time for them to come back into life again. Then they find themselves automatically drawn into the body of a fetus. Sometimes these people seem to have little choice about the conditions of their new life, as others do. In the transcripts below, Carol's illustrates this kind of interlife experience.

Both of these scenarios are very different from the familiar NDE I described above. As mentioned earlier, clients who are not directly guided into the NDE do not usually report it, and another researcher in past-life regression, Robert James, who also does not direct people into the NDE, finds the same two scenarios I described above. Many physicians have speculated that the NDE is the result of extreme stress on the brain, such as oxygen deprivation, carbon dioxide overload, or some brain chemical imbalance caused by severe physical trauma. Both Robert James and I, and other past life therapists who do not direct clients into the NDE, agree with them.

There is one group of people who report a still different interlife experience: agoraphobics, who often report the "lost soul" interlife experience I discussed in Chapter 4. According to their Upper Minds, this lost soul interlife experience actually caused their agoraphobia. So far as I know, this is the only kind of interlife experience that causes problems, and the only problem it seems to cause is agoraphobia.

I described this lost soul interlife experience in Chapter 4, on Phobias, since it is unique to agoraphobics; it was first described by Dr. Marianne de Jong. The most important elements of the lost soul interlife experience seem to be that the person had a confusing time of floating helplessly and aimlessly after their death in the prior life, and that they never realized they had died before beginning the present life. Another common factor is that usually the person had died either very suddenly or in a state of unconsciousness. In Chapter 4, I describe two such cases, one of a man who had been struck by lightning, the other of a woman who had died in a coma during an illness.

However, this does not happen to all who die in these circumstances; many people die suddenly or when unconscious and they do not experience this lost soul interlife. Instead, they know they have died and experience one of the more usual interlife experiences above. So this kind of death does not automatically produce a lost soul interlife (and perhaps an agoraphobic in the next life). The deciding factor may be whether or not the person realizes that he or she has died. But why some people should realize this, after the same death conditions, and agoraphobics do not, is just one of the many mysteries of past-life regressions.

The excerpts below are from audiotapes of four clients' interlife experiences. Betty's experience represents the first interlife experience I described above, and is the more usual interlife experience that clients report. Carol's experience of light is not typical, but her sense of not being ready to come back is not so unusual. However, she did not meet any "group," and in this her experience is typical of the second regular interlife experience I described above. The third and fourth transcript excerpts are from two women with agoraphobia, Marge and Marian, and represent two slightly different lost soul interlife experiences.

BETTY

Betty, the client with the phobia for caterpillars I discussed in Chapter 4, had a happy experience during the interlife before her present life, even a jolly one, and she was ready to come back. She had a turnaround time of eleven years from her death as John. Betty saw light imagery, and uses the concept of "meeting at the light," although she had not been drawn to a light to find her "group." Excerpts from her regression follow.

T: . . . it's before you're born, just before you join the fetus, a little way before—So I'm going to ask you, where are you? Are you still floating?

B: I'm talking to people. I'm talking to people [laughs].

T: Okay. Who're you talking to?

B: I don't know *[laughs]*.

T: Okay, who are they? Are they helping you decide?

B: Yeah *[laughs]*.

T: Are they your group?

B: I don't know who they are. "Oh you go, oh you go" *[laughs]*.

T: In other words, someone has to go and you're going to be it, huh? *[She laughs]* Don't they want to?

B: No.

T: I see.

B: No, they don't mind.

T: Mm-hm. But you're sort of it this time, is that right?

B: Uh-huh.

T: Okay. How do you feel about it?

B: I don't mind it.

T: Okay. Are you making any arrangements with anybody there to meet you, to meet up, get to know each other in any way in the life experience?

B: No—they'll meet back at the light.

T: They'll meet back at the light. That's your group, isn't it.

B: It's funny that you don't remember when you're—you remember at the—at that stage, when you're in the light you remember, but not during the lifetime.

T: Mm-hm. Why is that?

B: I don't know.

T: Do you think it's better that way?

B: I guess you would live differently.

T: Would you?

B: *[Pause]* This is very interesting. You wouldn't mind all the little things that went on.

T: Mm-hm. Like caterpillars?

B: Isn't that funny. I guess not. Because everybody's going to go back to that—to the light. How can I explain it? It seems to me like after you die, you get to this all-encompassing light area, and you sit around with everybody, and enjoy yourself, and that's the real life. And then you take turns going back—back into the world.

T: But you have reasons for coming into the world. What are your reasons? What are you going to accomplish this time around?

B: *[Long pause]* Who are you talking to? Betty?

T: Mm-hm—or is there another name I should use? Am I talking to your Upper Mind?

B: *[Pause]* What did I always want to accomplish? I always wanted to be an artist.

T: Is that one of the things that perhaps as Betty you'll be able to accomplish?

B: Yes.

T: Okay. That's a pretty good goal.

B: And I'm going to start soon *[laughs]*.

T: Okay. I believe it. You will.

(She did, too, and has become a member of several local art groups and sells her paintings.)

One interesting moment in this interlife experience, and one of the reasons I chose this one to discuss here, is when Betty said, "Who are you talking to? Betty?" I realized immediately that this was Betty's Upper Mind talking to me. When it speaks directly, it uses the third person when referring to the person. The voice was also somewhat different, more detached. I preferred at that moment to continue talking with Betty herself directly, but I accepted the shift and asked, "Am I talking to your Upper Mind?" After a pause, however, Betty, as Betty herself and not her Upper Mind, answered the question I had asked before this little detour. But I knew that if her Upper Mind had really wanted to continue talking to me directly, it would have done so regardless of my preference or Betty's either.

Betty referred to an "all-encompassing light area"; as you will see in the next transcript, Carol felt drawn through an opening like a "door" in the light that drew her against her will back into life again. And although Carol felt she was not ready, Betty seemed ready enough, if somewhat grudging about the prospect!

CAROL

T: Just letting yourself float up into that time, after you died as Ambrose and before you were born as Carol—Leaving Ambrose's body now, and feeling calm, okay. Three-two-one-zero. Where are you?

C: It's—space.

T: Space. Can you feel your body, do you have a body?

C: Somewhat.

T: Mm-hm. Can you see anything?

C: No.

T: All right. Is it black, dark, or light around you?

C: I'm beginning to see light.

T: Beginning to see light. What kind of light?

C: Yellow.

T: Okay, yellow. Just flow along there, and you can talk to me about it. Just let it happen.

C: I see shadows of figures.

T: Shadows of figures. Who are they?

C: I don't know, they're people.

T: People you know?

C: No.

T: All right. Anyone you know?

C: No.

T: Keep moving along, moving forward in time.

C: I see—it's like the light has streaks in it, and somebody walks through it, opens a door, and shuts the door.

T: Really? What kind of a door?

C: It's just a—a space.

T: Who walked through?

C: One of the shadows. The door—it—really it isn't a door, it's just an opening in the light and then the shadow goes through. And then the light covers the opening and the opening isn't there anymore.

T: Are you going to go through that opening?

C: No.

T: Why not?

C: It's not mine.

T: It's not yours? What does that mean?

C: I don't want to.

T: You don't want to. All right. What do you want to do instead?

C: Walk into the light.

T: Walk into the light?

C: Bright light, very very bright.

T: Very bright. How do you feel?

C: A little scared.

T: Mm-hm.

C: It's just—intense. I keep expecting to feel heat, but there isn't any.

T: There isn't any. Okay. Is that because of the brightness of the light?

C: Yeah, it's almost white.

T: But there isn't any heat?

C: No.

T: Okay. Are you going to go through the light?

C: Yeah, but I can't conceive of it. I keep expecting to touch a lightbulb [laughs].

T: Well, let yourself just flow.

C: And I go through the light, and I fall.

T: And you fall? Where?

C: I see my parents' house.

T: You see your parents' house. And where are you?

C: Where am I?

T: When you see your parents' house.

C: Um—inside of it.

T: You're inside of it?

C: Mm-hm.

T: Do they know you're there?

C: Hm-mm [no].

T: Okay. Where are you inside?

C: In their, uh—I'm not ready to be there yet.

T: You're not ready to be there yet? Okay. Why did you choose them?

C: Just happened.

T: Just happened. You didn't choose?

C: Well—I went through the light and I was there.

T: Mm-hm, you went through the light and then you were there. Well, go back to the time before you went through the light.

C: Well, shadows were going through openings.

T: The shadows were going through—

C: Dark openings, though.

T: Mm-hm. When you went through the light, was it a dark opening?

C: No, it was very bright.

T: And then you just fell?

C: It was almost like they were in the light.

T: Like who was in the light?

C: My parents.

T: Mm-hm. Were they?

C: Yeah, they were in the light, or they were the light, because I could feel them.

T: And you found yourself then in the house. But you said it wasn't time yet, you weren't ready yet?

C: Yeah.

T: Or they weren't ready for you, which?

C: I see the house, they were in the light, they wanted me, but I wasn't ready.

T: You weren't ready?

C: For them.

T: Mm-hm. You mean you came before you were ready?

C: Yeah.

Carol reported seeing bright light, but it was a bright light that led her into her birth, and did not appear immediately after her death in the past life. Carol also set no personal goals. She said later that she came back to fill someone else's need, her father's, not her own.

T: Now thinking back, and I'm talking now to your Upper Mind, thinking over all your past lives, have you known one of your parents or both of them before in another life? Just let it flow.

C: My dad.

T: Mm-hm—which life?

C: I don't know, but—he is in pain.

T: He was in pain?

C: He is in pain.

T: Become aware of the incident, the time, the place, that you knew him before, very calmly.

C: Can't—*[long pause]*.

T: How did you know he was in pain?

C: I could feel it.

T: You could feel his pain?

C: I could feel it through the light.

T: All right. He was in pain, mentally or physically?

C: Mentally. They both needed me.

T: Why did they both need you?

C: They needed another person.

T: They needed another person. Why?

C: I can feel my mother needing the other person too. Because they were frightened.

T: What were they frightened of?

C: They were frightened of dying. They were frightened of life.

T: Just with the two of them?

C: Yeah. They were frightened of being grown up.

T: And did you—you had the feeling that you had known your father before?

C: Briefly, just briefly.

T: Do you know where? Or when?

C: No.

T: Think about—you say briefly. How do you know it was briefly?

C: It was an acquaintance, in, uh—

T: It'll come.

C: *[Pause]* The university, the—Miguelo's university.

T: Which university?

C: Miguelo's.

T: Miguelo's, Okay. And where was that?

C: In New Spain.

T: In New Spain, Okay. And he was just an acquaintance. You were there and he was there too?

C: Yeah, he was like a casual friend of mine. I liked him a lot. And he had gotten himself into this space of insecurities and, uh,—I liked him before a lot, he was sort of spontaneous and a lot of energy and a lot of ideas, and he seemed trapped in this place.

T: So you were glad to go to him? You felt safe and that it would
be fun?

C: Mm-hm.

Carol really seemed to have no choice in the matter. She was
simply drawn in, through a "door" in the light, and although she
was afraid, and knew she was not ready, she went, automatically
drawn to help a friend from a lifetime in which both had died in
the sixteenth century. Carol examined all fourteen of her past
lives, including the Ambrose and Miguelo lives, mentioned in the
transcript excerpts above; I discuss these in detail in Chapter 13.

Carol's turnaround time of eight years is shorter than average
for this century, which is about twelve to fifteen years. Betty's, of
eleven years, is closer to the average. The length of time between
lives seems to be shortening in this century. This may be because
there are so many more people being born and therefore it is easier to be reborn than it used to be: there are always plenty of fe-
tuses getting ready to be born. But short turnaround times may
also mean that a good many of us come in with more leftover business to finish than if we had waited longer. The late Dr. Russell
Davis, a past-life therapist, once pointed out that many people who
died during World War II seem to have returned now, and many of
them returned after short turnaround times with unfinished business and problems related to their experiences during that war. As
he said, all past-life therapists have noticed this.

The question of when people actually join the fetus is an interesting one. Most say they join the fetus from about three or four
months before birth to immediately before the birth. I have even
known a client to say she floated in and out of the fetus's body for
three or four months before birth but then left the little body during the birth itself and drifted above the scene because she "hated
being born." This client said she always did that, and rejoined the
baby's body after "things settle down." All this has a direct bearing
on the abortion debate in the United States. From the evidence of
past-life regressions, an abortion during the first trimester would
seem to be an abortion of a fetus with "nobody home" yet, one not
yet inhabited by anyone.

Carol answers the question of joining the body in a way both sad and amusing:

T: At what point are you going to join your body?

C: Right before I'm born.

T: Right before you're born? Now have you been hanging around there?

C: Yeah.

T: Why did you wait?

C: I didn't want to be inside of her *[laughs]*.

T: You didn't want to be inside of her? Why not?

C: *[Laughs]* Sounds gross, doesn't it.

T: Why not? Just in general, you don't like that feeling, or just her?

C: Yeah, I'm not too thrilled with her.

T: With her. Well, okay. Now you're going to join the body. How do you do that?

C: Well, I don't know. I make a—you know I feel that—being inside now.

T: Are you comfortable being in that body?

C: No.

T: Why? Too small for you?

C: Yeah.

T: Okay. I'm going to count from three to zero and quickly past the point of your birth—

C: I also feel—

T: You also feel what?

C: Like I can't breathe.

T: Yeah, well, let's take care of that. Okay, three-two-one-zero, okay, now you're born and you can breathe.

C: Yeah. I feel like, uh—this body is so fragile, and, uh, like the—like I'm starving.

T: For what?

C: Food.

T: Mm-hm, okay.

C: And I also feel, uh—*[pause]*.

T: I want you to experience a moment of love, protection, tenderness, from your mother—welcoming.

C: [Laughs] She's a fairly—she can't express herself *[laughs]*.

T: Can you accept that okay?

C: Yeah.

T: And experience a moment like that with your father, welcoming.

C: He's glad I'm here.

T: Mm-hm. Are you going to be all right?

C: Yeah, I guess.

T: Mm-hm, I think so too.

Both Carol and Betty had set goals before they were born. For Carol, it was an almost automatic goal, to fill her father's need and heal his pain, although she seemed to have little or no choice in the matter. But Betty's goal, to become an artist, was chosen by Betty herself before she was born. Of the two, Betty's goal seems more productive and more apt to lead to a good life than Carol's. But Carol also said that she had a past-life connection with her father, so she may have been working out some old relationship issue, although she does not say so. It is more as if she was simply drawn to help an old friend in trouble.

People say they have a variety of goals for the coming life. One client said he wanted to develop a talent for healing that he had begun in his most recent life; another, to teach children; a third, to have a family and learn to live in close relationship with others. Still others say the opposite: They plan to learn to live more independently than they have in earlier lives. And some have issues that need to be straightened out with someone else; they may choose the "someone else" as a parent or other relative in the coming life, as Carol did.

People do not always choose their parents or any other particular person to return to or with: Carol chose her father, although automatically, but Betty made no such specific choice. Later in her session Betty said that she had chosen a couple who seemed to be happy, because she felt they would give her a happy, stable family to grow up in, and they had. But she had no past-life relationship with them. I discussed various relationship choices involved in past lives in Chapter 7.

When people make some choice about the life circumstances they are entering, it is usually some old relationship or personal attribute of the parents upon which they base their choice. They also choose their goals for the coming life, as we have seen. But there are some things they never seem to choose. I have never heard a client say he or she is setting a goal to be wealthy, or to have power over others, or to become famous. Goals always have to do with working out a prior relationship, or learning something new, or continuing something begun in a past life, or learning some life skill such as how to love, to be happy in a family, or conversely, to be happy and independent. Goals have to do with learning to live life well. Even clients who are stuck in negative patterns set useful goals for themselves before they are born. They may not reach them, or even get started on them, because of their upbringing or the negative, destructive pattern, but they usually did set some useful goal before they were born.

Nor have I ever heard a client say that he or she was choosing a fetus of a particular gender or skin color. This seems to be of no importance whatsoever: People take what they get. This is rather interesting, because in our culture we are so gender- and race-identified. But these identifications seem to be something that the culture itself teaches us. It is possible that we need to have past-life experience as both genders in order to build good relationships with both men and women and understand the gender opposite to us now, in our present lives. The same may be true for skin color. But when we make our choices and plans for our coming life, and when we are born, gender and color are not part of those choices, at least not with my clients.

Much of what I have said above does not seem to apply to the agoraphobics who report the lost soul interlife experience, in which they do not even know they have died in one life and are entering another. Thus, they have not made any choices or set any goals for the coming life. They are simply drawn into the body of a fetus and born, still "caught" in the prior life, with no awareness that the past-life person has died. A good example of this experience is Marge's, although she is not floating through a dark place but rather through a mist of light. In response to my request that her Upper Mind take her in the magic chair to the source of her agoraphobia, Marge found herself floating through this mist.

MARGE

M: It's light.

T: It's light? What's light?

M: Everything.

T: Everything's light—and where are you?

M: I don't know.

T: You don't know—

M: Floating around—So light—

T: Is it just one light or all around?

M: All around.

T: Okay—follow through, become aware of what you did—what did you do next?

M: Hallway?

T: Hallway? Okay, let that flow—

M: Looks like a hospital—

T: Looks like a hospital—okay—what happens next—

M: I'm little—very little.

T: You're little again, huh? A baby or—

M: I think so *[laughs]*.

T: Okay—become aware of that—

M: I don't recognize anything—

T: You don't recognize anything—okay—were you just born?

M: Mm-hm.

T: Okay—become aware of that, get a hug from your mom and
    dad—how does that feel?

M: Good.

Later in the session Marge realized that she had died in the
prior life and she saw an "old woman sleeping in a bed," but she
did not yet identify with the woman. We continued:

T: Okay. But now go back to that previous life, though, when
    you came out and were floating around—did you realize that
    you had died in that lifetime?

M: No.

T: You didn't know it, huh? Okay. Now go back into that life-
    time, and this time—become aware of how you died in that
    lifetime.

M: She was real old.

T: Real old—what was her name? *[Pause, no answer]* But she was
    very old, huh?

M: Mm.

T: Did she die in her bed or what?

M: Mm—in bed.

T: Was she thinking straight, was her mind okay?

M: Hm [she is not sure].

T: Okay—and what happened? Very calmly, become aware of why that person died—

M: Sleeping.

T: Sleeping—she died in her sleep? So she wasn't aware when she died?

M: No.

T: Okay—was she aware that she had died in that lifetime?

M: No.

T: Okay—just imagine yourself now going back into that time after she died, and yourself now moving on forward, and then what happened next?

M: Home.

T: Home—and—as Marge or someone else?

M: Baby.

T: So is the baby Marge?

M: Mm.

T: Okay, now go back again now, to that old woman lying on her bed—now when you found yourself—suddenly everything was light all around, how did you feel about that? Was it scary?

M: No.

T: Comfortable?

M: Mm-hm.

T: And as you moved into this life as Marge, had you had time to make a plan, or a goal?

M: No.

T: Okay—so go back again, leaving that old woman's body, but this time find your people, your group, the time before you come in as Marge—let your Upper Mind guide you—

M: Back home [she meant into the baby's body again].

T: Okay.

It took several more shifts back and forth before Marge recognized that the old woman in the bed was her own past-life body and that she had actually died. It is noteworthy that in this excerpt, when Marge first refers to the woman in the bed, she switches to the third person. ("She was real old.") She has not identified with that woman yet, and I follow her lead by continuing to use the third person. This is typical of the lost soul interlife experience. Marge later finally did identify with her, and then I directed her back into the past life and we examined it like any other past life. I brought her through the death experience and this time instructed her to "do it right" and she managed to do that.

Although Marge's transition into the baby's body seems to have been immediate, the dates we finally got for this past life indicate that the turn-around time was actually over fifty years. But no clients, whether agoraphobic or not, are aware of the amount of time spent in the interlife, of whatever kind.

Marian, another agoraphobic, reported a slightly different lost soul interlife, and a more typical one for an agoraphobic:

MARIAN

T: . . . where are you?

M: I'm in dark fog, looking down.

T: You're looking down—what are you looking down on?

M: I'm looking down on—uh, the shoreline, looking down on—from high up—

T: Okay—now go back to the moment when you first got up there, go back to that moment—

M: My body has its back to the sky and its front toward the ground and I'm looking and I'm thinking this is not right, this should not have happened [she is speaking here of her "soul" body, floating over the scene below].

T: Okay—where is your body?

M: It's in the air—but it's just there looking down, it's in a dark place.

T: Okay—is it in the air or in the water?

M: Not—I guess it's in the air because—I'm looking down and thinking this should not have happened.

T: You mean your body that you're in, you're in the air?

M: Yes.

T: Okay—well, look at the body you left, before you started to float—

M: *[Pause]* That's the one laying on the beach, curled up.

T: That's the one laying on the beach curled up?

M: Yeah.

T: Okay—was it washed up on the beach or just there—

M: Um—I don't know.

T: When did you leave it?

M: On the beach I left it.

T: On the beach—

M: Yeah.

T: After you left that body on the beach, what did you do?

M: I was just feeling that—I don't know—

T: Did you know that you were dead?

M: I was just sad—I was—sad and helpless feeling—I feel helpless to help her—

T: So did you try?

M: Did I try what?

T: Try to help her?

M: No—just stuck there, feeling helpless—

T: Okay—now let's go forward to the next important thing that happens *[long pause]*.

M: I have to try again.

T: You have to try again?

M: Yeah—to make it right.

Marian, at the end of her interlife wanderings, suddenly recognized her true state and that she had to "try again" to "make it right." In the past life she had just left, she had been a woman who had drowned, but when we entered the experience above, we did not know that: Marian merely saw a woman's body down below on a beach. Like Marge, she referred to this body in the third person: "I feel helpless to help her." But then suddenly Marian recognized that she had left that body, and had to "try again to make it right."

The interlife experience, of any kind, is usually a profound one for people. Obviously, it takes away the fear of death, and this is a very freeing thing. As Carol hovered above her parents, she said, "They were frightened of dying. They were frightened of life. They were frightened of being grown up." Sadly, these three fears often go together, and they are common in our society. Experiencing the interlife wipes these fears away.

It also seems to leave people with a wider sense of themselves. As Betty commented in the transcript above, if people remembered the interlife after they were born, "You wouldn't mind all the little things that went on." After the interlife experience, clients seem to approach life with a sense of adventure, of humor, and of enjoyment of life for its own sake, as well as a new resolve to meet the goals they came in with.

Even for agoraphobics, after exploring the strange lost soul interlife, they realize that they died in the prior life and entered a new one, and that they must now, as Marian said, "Make it right."

Before I work with a client, and before I begin a workshop, I warn people that exploring their past lives for any reason will change them whether they think so in advance or not. The interlife experience is a major reason for this change.

As I said above, Carol and I examined all fourteen of her past lives, and in the next chapter I discuss them in detail.

CHAPTER THIRTEEN

ONE WOMAN'S PAST LIVES

What does one person's complete series of past lives look like, from the first life to the most recent one? Oddly, there has been no such complete series published before. This may be because most past lives are examined in connection with therapy for specific problems, and although a given problem, for example a phobia or a difficult relationship, may be related to two or three past lives, it is most likely not related to all the other lives that the client may have lived. Therefore, those other lives are not examined in the usual course of past-life therapy. I have a few complete series of past lives; below, I discuss Carol's as being a typical series. Carol's Upper Mind said she had lived fourteen past lives, and we examined them all.

We examined them at a leisurely pace, one per session, with sessions two or more weeks apart. In some cases, more than one session was devoted to one past life, if we seemed to have missed something important the first time. Except for the first we examined, the "Elsa" life, we examined the past lives in whatever order her Upper Mind chose. But for the Elsa life, I gave Carol's Upper Mind direct instructions to take her back to one of her past lives that she "would enjoy remembering." This is a useful, nonthreatening beginning to such a series. In every other session, I asked her Upper Mind to lead us into the past life "that should be examined next," and this led us wandering through time and place in a nonchronological order. Nevertheless, after all of her past lives had been examined and Carol and I arranged them chronologically, we found that there were no overlapping dates. I present them here in chronological order, because by so doing the processes of growth that she experienced through her past lives can be most clearly seen. And after all, chronologically is the order in which Carol actually lived these lives, if she did at all.

I have done a certain amount of historical research to see if the lives Carol reported were plausible, both in general outlines and in details. In past-life work, it often happens that something reported by a client seems historically impossible, and then when it is checked, it turns out to be not only possible but likely.

This sort of research is not easy. I have checked a lot of past-life narratives, and one thing I have learned is humility about my knowledge of history. It is no help, either, that history books tend to focus on wars, politics, and great social shifts and changes: They skip blithely over whole centuries and "unimportant" areas of the world. And they may tell me the reign dates, wars, and court intrigues of Roman emperors, but they tell me nothing about what a poor woman in that same long-ago Rome might prepare for her family's supper, or how she would prepare it.

Past-life narratives are often located in times or places that are obscure and not easily found in history books, and the people of past lives are also usually obscure, ordinary people, so this kind of research can require a lot of ferreting out of dusty tomes from forgotten library shelves, and sometimes details are not to be found at all. Fortunately, at the time I worked with Carol, I had access to the miraculous dusty shelves of the libraries of New York City, so checking for plausibility was not as difficult as it might have been. What I could, I checked, and plausibility was established for all of these past lives in their general outlines, and for many details as well. Other details I could not find recorded, although given the conditions of the lives, they, too, seem plausible. None of the past-life people themselves were famous nor are they mentioned in any book or film that I know about. I have included some of the findings of my researches in the descriptions of the past lives when those findings make understanding the life easier.

I need not discuss the specific problems that brought Carol to therapy, except in general terms, where these might be relevant to the sequence of past lives she reported. What I want to focus on here is that sequence.

All of these past lives were facilitated by a fairly deep level of hypnosis. Carol is an excellent hypnosis subject who reaches deep levels rapidly. She also accesses clear and detailed images easily, with little prompting from me. The names of the past-life people were given by Carol herself in hypnosis. Usually she could "hear" others use the past-life character's first name when I directed her to do so. Some she heard clearly, others indistinctly, and some were partly guessed at. Unfamiliar names are spelled phonetically, by Carol herself.

As for the dates given, Carol's Upper Mind was asked to place the year of death and the age at which the past-life person died "in modern terms" on an imaginary screen "like a TV screen" after the past life had been explored; I always ask for this information "in modern terms" so it is comprehensible to the person and myself. The names of the geographical locations were gathered in the same way, as "what we call the place now." As I said in an earlier chapter, this technique seems less like an intrusion than to ask directly during the regression itself, and in any case the person will become confused and guess at answers if asked directly during the actual regression.

CAROL

Carol was a woman in her early thirties, a graduate student at a large university, married, with a young daughter. Her Upper Mind said she had lived a total of fourteen prior lives, and we examined them all. Each character was a distinct personality, living a realistic life for the time and place. These fourteen lives included nine male and five female lives of varying nationalities and religious systems, three or four skin colors, and were lived on five different continents. None were famous or especially powerful people in their cultures. Carol's fourteen lives span just over two thousand years, with no overlapping dates given.

CAROL'S FOURTEEN PAST LIVES

Ker, 134 B.C.E..–104 B.C.E, Italy

Chronologically, Carol's first life was as a man, "Ker-[something]." Ker was born in what we know as 134 B.C.E., a member of a small, peaceful group living along the coast of Italy. This group was fairly primitive and sounded like one of the small lingering tribes gradually being assimilated by Rome at that time. Because of a probably parasitic disease that slowly deformed his body, Ker had difficulty walking and was never entirely accepted by his people. He lived a lonely life, dying of his disease at thirty. He was a simple soul who made himself as useful as possible to his group, and never seemed to realize that he was lonely. In fact, Carol said she had learned "humor and just to enjoy living" in that lifetime.

Ben, C.E.170–210, Scotland

Carol's second life was also a male life, as "Ben," born in C.E. 170. Ben was a "rough" warrior in a rather savage Pict or Scot tribe in the hills of what we know as Scotland. He died at forty, in 210, of a wound from a spear through his stomach in a battle with another tribe. Ben was a jolly sort, married, had children, and had a position of some influence in his group. In that lifetime Carol said she learned some things about leadership, and how to fit in with other people.

Suki, 220–283, Sri Lanka

Carol's third life, as "Suki," was a female. Suki was born in 220 in Sri Lanka (Carol saw "Ceylon" on the screen). Suki's mother was killed by her father shortly after Suki's birth, possibly because he questioned whether or not he was Suki's true father, although Suki was not sure about that. Tossed into the bushes after her mother's murder, the baby Suki was rescued by her maternal grandfather and raised by him. He taught her to play a stringed instrument and to dance, and when Suki was fifteen, she became a member of a group of musicians and dancers who entertained at festivals and private celebrations. Suki never married but had a son. Hers was a happy life while she was young, but in later life, apparently abandoned by her son and with all her friends gone, her mind seemed to have deserted her. Old, sick, wandering, and starving, she gorged on some raw rice she found and died. In this Suki life, Carol said she had learned to love music and dancing, but another lesson was that you couldn't depend on friends or even your own child and that a lonely old age was terrible.

Marcus, 550–601, Tunis (Carthage) and Rome

"Marcus," another male life, was Carol's fourth. Born in 550 in Tunisia (then Carthage) of a Carthaginian mother and a Roman officer, at three or four Marcus was taken to Rome by his father, leaving his mother in Carthage. He never went back and never saw her again. This did not bother Marcus one whit. When I asked him if he had ever gone back to see her, he was puzzled by my question, asked me why he would do that, and rather arrogantly declared that "she was just a physical mother."

In Rome, Marcus was raised and well educated in his father's well-to-do household. He married and had children. But during Marcus's lifetime his family's estates were confiscated, Marcus himself was impoverished, and he was eventually executed in 601, when he was fifty-one. Carol said that in this life she had learned "how to use my mind, how to live only through ideas." Although this was true for Marcus, who was very intellectual, in the end his opinions were the cause of his death.

When I researched this past life, I found that during Marcus's time the Eastern (Christian) Empire was retaking the Western Empire from the Goths, who had encouraged religious freedom, and those Roman families who refused to convert to approved forms of Christianity were destroyed. Apparently Marcus belonged to such a family. He said that his crime was that he refused to acknowledge the divinity of the Emperor, and I found that this was one of the major controversies of the time and was grounds for execution.

Shad, 664–709, Spain

Carol's fifth life was as "Shad," born in Spain in 664 into a small seminomadic group where he became a blacksmith. In his adolescence, while learning his trade from his grandfather, Shad had made strange humanlike figures of iron "to see what I could do." He married and had children, becoming a respected member of his community. However, when he was forty-five years old, the old strange figures were discovered and the community found them impious by the local religious standards. Shad's hands were amputated and he chose to be left to die in a desert area rather than be dependent upon his family. Carol said that in this life she had learned the importance of finding the right people to live among and that organized religious beliefs can be very cruel and narrow-minded.

El, 817–ca.900, Egypt

"El-[something]," a woman born in 817 in Egypt, was Carol's sixth life. El was singularly unresponsive to events, and Carol herself, during the regression, suddenly "moved out of character" and announced that El was probably mentally retarded. El was raised by an uncle in an Egyptian city; she did not know what had happened to her parents. When she was nine, her uncle sold her to a house of prostitution in a "market town" farther south and east along the Nile. (Terrible as this might seem to us, it was not unusual for the time and place, and may have seemed the only logical thing for the uncle to do with this mentally retarded, orphaned, or abandoned niece.) El had no particular objection to her new life. However, she left there at around fifteen, when a catastrophe involving terrible heat and falling ash killed many of the townspeople and forced her to flee. (This sounds like an eruption of one of the volcanoes along the western Red Sea, still alive today.) Eventually wandering to a nearby village, El made herself useful by doing domestic chores for the village women, who fed her and let her sleep in their houses in return for her work. El died there as an "old woman," probably of a heart attack, while carrying water in the village street. In this life Carol said she had learned "how to remain sane and to not get involved, how to survive without feelings, without anything, without any love." Sad lessons, indeed.

Shal, 1087–1102, India/Pakistan

Carol's seventh life was as "Shal-[something]," born in 1087 along what is today the India-Pakistan border, the son and heir of a prosperous man with estates that were mostly jungle. Well raised in a loving family, when he was fifteen his father and then he himself were murdered by his father's brothers, who thus inherited the estates. Shal had had plans for the land and he was angry at this early murder: "I never had a chance," he says. In this lifetime, Carol said she had learned not to be passive, to "look out for myself." She said that if Shal had been more alert and assertive, he might have become aware of his uncles' plot against him, especially after they murdered his father, and he could have prevented his own murder.

Margarite, 1380/90–1452, England

"Margarite," as Carol's eighth life, was born in England in the late fourteenth century. Raised on a farm, she lived a busy life, marrying a farmer-carpenter and very capably raising their many children. Margarite grew a great deal during her life. When she married, she was an uncertain, insecure girl, marrying a man she did not particularly care for, but over the years she grew into a happy, secure wife and mother and built a good relationship with her husband. After a long and happy life, she died in bed with her family around her, an "old woman," in 1452. Carol said that as Margarite she had learned to communicate, to share her thoughts and worries. Margarite said that it was through talking together that she and her husband eventually became good friends and partners.

Miguelo, 1475–1527, Spain, New Spain (Caribbean Islands)

"Miguelo," as Carol's ninth life, was born in Spain in 1475 and raised in a convent by nuns, one of whom may have been his mother. Miguelo entered a monastery but left in his late twenties, moving to a university city where he continued his studies and taught as a lay brother. He married and fathered a daughter, raising her successfully after his wife died. Miguelo moved to New Spain after those colonies were established in the early 1500s, continuing to teach there. Miguelo's death, in 1527 when he was fifty-two, was unusual. He seems to have died in his sleep from a heart attack caused by a nightmare in which he dreamed that a hooded figure crept into his room and smothered him. The hooded figure might have been real, but Carol, as Miguelo, said it was not, it was part of his nightmare. In that lifetime, Carol said she had learned "to be able to deal with death—to accept its being with you." In Chapter 12, I discussed Carol's interlife experience and her choice of her present father, who had been a friend of Miguelo's in New Spain. But we do not know which friend he was.

Marcel, 1541–1601, England and the Canary Islands

Carol's tenth life was as "Marcel," born in 1541 in England, in a small town somewhere along the coast. Marcel was a colorful character who was no better than he needed to be. Raised a "poor boy," he began his career by running errands for men selling contraband and smuggled goods. By his thirties he was selling smuggled gunpowder to dissident groups, but eventually he found the gunpowder business "too risky" and started instead a business of "moving spices" and "other things." Marcel was rather evasive about what "other things" he "moved." (Marcel was evasive about many things; he clearly did not quite trust me!) He somehow acquired a ship of his own and settled in the Canary Islands, a haunt of pirates of the day, where he married (his chuckles about this word made me think he had not really married, but he said he had). In any case, his "wife" had red hair and a lively temper, both of which Marcel much admired. They successfully raised a sprawling family of five. Marcel seems not to have been a pirate himself but instead "carried and sold goods." He died on his ship in 1601 at sixty, of an illness or, possibly, from poisoning by a "business rival." Carol said she had learned "how to be independent, how to make my own way, how to be assertive" in her life as Marcel.

When I checked, I found that the Canary Islands were centers for merchants who sold pirated goods. The merchants had their own ships and met the pirates in the Scilly Islands, where the stolen goods were sold to them and transferred to their ships, then carried back to their shops in the Canaries or other colonized islands. Marcel seems to have been such a merchant: today we would call him a "fence."

Antoinette, 1704–1754, England

"Antoinette," as Carol's eleventh life, was born in the Lake District of England in 1704. Raised there by her grandparents, she had a love of singing and moved to London in her teens, where she became a singer in London clubs. She was a "joyous person" who loved her singing, pretty clothes, and fancy hats. "Not exactly a prostitute," as she makes very clear, she established a long-term relationship (nonsexual, she says) with a music-loving widower and raised his three children. However, after his death and after the children had grown, she went back to the Lake District. Nearly penniless, she cleaned houses for a while, but finally, in 1754 when she was fifty, alone and depressed, she killed herself by drowning. In that life, Carol said, she had learned how to give to other people, how to love unselfishly, and how to nurture. She also said, when considering Antoinette's suicide, that she had learned "to give life a chance, to wait and see what happens next."

Jean-Pierre, 1764–1801, England and France

"Jean-Pierre," as Carol's twelfth life, was born "John Peter" in England in 1764, the son of a prosperous farm family. In his early teens he ran away from home and went to Paris, drawn by the rhetoric of prerevolutionary France. Well educated, he found work with a printer, eventually owning a printing shop of his own, marrying, and fathering a child. He was financially successful but remained a political critic and activist. Finally in 1801, during a purge of dissident printers in Napoleon's dictatorship, he was imprisoned and then guillotined, at thirty-seven. Carol said that she had learned "strength, independence, mind" in this lifetime.

Elsa, 1818–1864, New Orleans and Massachusetts

"Elsa" was Carol's thirteenth life. Elsa was born in 1818 in New Orleans and was of mixed races. She was her white father's favorite child and he encouraged her talent for drawing. In her late teens or early twenties, with his blessing and probably by his arrangement, she went north to friends in Massachusetts, a free state. Elsa does not say so, but after we discovered the dates for this life, I realized that if she had stayed in Louisiana she would, of course, legally have remained a slave. In Massachusetts she lived and worked in a community of workers designing and building machinery that was used in railroad building. This was a happy group and Elsa was content with her place in it; her work involved drafting of some sort. She married a fellow-worker but had no children; she died in 1864 of an illness.

This was the first past life Carol explored; I had given directions for her Upper Mind to take her back into one of her past lives that she "would enjoy remembering," and this life as Elsa was the one she went to. "It was a happy life," said Carol while still in hypnosis when I asked her Upper Mind why it had chosen this one. She said she had learned "how to be strong and independent, how to use my mind and my talents, but within a nurturing kind of atmosphere." Elsa said that all her life she had "had this knowledge that I was always going to be taken care of."

The workers' community in Massachusetts sounded far-fetched to me, but when I researched it, I found that Massachusetts was a center for railroad design and development and that the railroad companies set up numerous small workers' communities such as Elsa describes, and employed both men and women in them. The first railroad in the United States was Gridley Bryant's Granite Railway, built in Quincy, Massachusetts, in 1826 (when Elsa was eight years old). It was four miles long, used horse-drawn cars, and was built to carry the granite from the quarry to the site of the Bunker Hill Monument. During the following decades many such short railways were built throughout Massachusetts and New England. Eventually they were linked together and became the nucleus of our railroad system. I also found that there were many small, experimental utopian workers' communities such as Elsa describes in Massachusetts and to some extent the rest of New England. The railroad companies especially were leaders in these utopian experiments, in which the workers, both men and women, lived and worked together. In fact, the railroad companies were much criticized for their "soft" policies toward workers. The railroad companies may eventually have changed those policies, but in Elsa's time, things were as she says.

Ambrose, 1878–1945, Austria (?), England, and Belgium or France

Carol's fourteenth and most recent life was as a man, "Ambrose," and he was a tortured soul. Born in 1878, the youngest of three sons of a comfortable farm family, Ambrose was raised in a mountainous area of Europe, probably the Austrian Alps. He felt called to a spiritual and religious life from his early years and was sent to England to study, where he became a minister. During his seminary years he had an intense love affair that he himself ended as interfering with his "spirituality." He never had another close relationship with anyone, male or female.

His was not a happy life. The most introspective of Carol's past-life characters, Ambrose was increasingly troubled by the contradictions of religion and science, and eventually came to doubt the existence of God. He became an assistant to a country clergyman, but as time went by, he began to doubt his ability to help the people of the congregation with their problems, or even to care about them. He says:

> When I realized that the minister that I was working under didn't know any more than I knew—and was just interested in performing certain duties for a congregation—which I didn't feel part of—I couldn't feel emotionally enough for them to want to comfort them—and I didn't feel God was there any longer—I just decided that in that case, when I had no feeling for the people—it wasn't a hatred or anything but I just felt that I couldn't be useful—then I left.

Ambrose returned to Europe, either to France or Belgium, near the sea, where he purchased a small farm and began to keep bees, selling honey in the nearby towns. He became more and more reclusive, and came to prefer his bees to people: He talked to them as individuals, and toward the end "the sensuality of being around the bees was the most important thing." Sometimes at night he would sit on a small hill overlooking the sea and listen to the surf and "try to find God again." He never succeeded.

Ambrose may have gone a bit mad at the end. He began to imagine that the loved woman of his youth was "somewhere around," a shadowy figure just out of sight. At sixty-seven, in 1945, he died in bed of an illness, alone, with, as he says, a "war going on and a lot of unhappiness everywhere." Carol said that in this life she learned "to not lose my spirituality, to guard against losing it— the kind of spirituality I'm talking about is the excitement of life." And "the one thing is this sense of self, he was pretty solid throughout. Even though he went through some kind of dilemma, he solved it for himself."

Carol, who was born in New York State eight years after Ambrose's death, was astonished by the dilemmas of Ambrose. She had given religion scant thought and did not think of herself as a spiritual person. As an interesting sidelight, she commented that her parents had told her that as a small child she had horrified them by letting bees crawl on her arms and talking to them. They had never stung her, and despite her parents' frantic reactions in her childhood, she still found bees beautiful and had no fear of them.

This is not an unusual picture for people who report all of their past lives. What do we see in this chronology? For one thing, we see a growing richness and complexity of personality over the years from the first to the last of these fourteen past lives, and on to Carol as she is today. From the first life as "Ker," a simple tribesman in the Italian peninsula in the first century B.C.E., to the last as Ambrose, a complex clergyman of the present century, tortured by theological doubts and finally losing his faith entirely, we see the complexity of personality as it grows itself. And finally to Carol, born eight years after Ambrose's death and still wondering about the truth of the world, but no longer a believer in God. She had dropped this belief in her early teens, finding it irrelevant. After she explored the Ambrose life, she commented that she seemed to have already wrestled with "all that" as Ambrose.

A modern concern of Carol's, however, was the conflict she felt between being independent and dependent. Many of us sense this conflict: Being independent is risky and sometimes lonely, but being safely dependent on others can feel imprisoning to the free human being. Generally, we all agree that we must take the risk of some independence at least, of making our own choices and finding our own best way, and of building good relationships without undue dependence on other people. But in Carol's chain of lives, independence had sometimes led to loneliness and even to disaster.

For example, Suki was happy while she was a member of her little musical community, playing her instrument and living with the others, but in her old age she lost that community and died alone and friendless; even her son had somehow disappeared. Marcus and Jean-Pierre were independent and supported ideas that were at variance with the "establishment" of their day, and both were executed for it. On the other hand, Ben, Marcel, and Miguelo were very independent people and it worked for them. Throughout many of Carol's fourteen past lives, the themes of independence and dependence are played out in various ways.

It is as if Carol has been trying to find the right balance between these attributes for centuries, as perhaps many of us have been. Seeing these patterns in her past lives, however, enabled her to realize that she could choose the amount and kinds of independence she wanted and needed and still build good relationships.

Carol found other connections between her past lives and her present life. Some involved troubles: an old recurrent stomachache she had experienced all her life was suddenly briefly reexperienced as Ben died, fatally wounded by a spear through his stomach. After her regression to Ben, she has never had the pain again. Her fear of her own creativity was linked to Shad's life and death, in which Shad's hands were amputated because he had experimented creatively with forging human forms. A slight "nervousness" around knives was traced to Shal's murder by a knife and to Margarite's father's death by a knife wound. As the reader may surmise from Chapter 4, "Phobias," this looks like a phobia aborning. Shal and Margarite lived centuries ago, but one more bad experience with knives, in a more recent life, and Carol might have had a full-blown knife phobia. Or it may have been solidified in this present life or a future one. Perhaps by examining these two past lives at this stage we nipped a phobia in the bud. At any rate, Carol no longer has her "nervousness" around knives.

Some connections were positive. We know from her interlife experience that she chose her present father because he had been Miguelo's friend in that life, although we do not know which friend. Carol's creativity itself, her talent for art, and her love for music were traced to Suki's playing and dancing, Antoinette's love of music and singing, and Elsa's love of drawing. And like Antoinette, Carol still loves pretty clothes and music. Her love for children was traced to many lives: Ben, Suki, Antoinette, Margarite, Miguelo, and Marcel all loved their children deeply and nurturingly. I have mentioned her admiration for bees, apparently a holdover from the Ambrose life. And her tendency toward independent political thought as well as her proclivity to "push the limits," to do something different (for example, to investigate all of her past lives), was linked with her Marcus, Marcel, Antoinette, and Jean-Pierre lives.

Carol reported nine male and five female lives. As I said in Chapter 12, one thing that people seem not to "choose" when making the decision to be reborn is what gender they will be. Other things seem important in this choice, but not gender. Nor is skin color chosen. Carol did not choose her gender or her skin color in any of these past lives, or in her present life either.

One thing that emerges from Carol's series of fourteen past lives is that problems such as Carol's conflicts about independence and dependence or her other problems can be caused by cumulative experiences in past lives. As we have seen, many problems are found to be caused by clients' past lives, and becoming aware of those causes usually relieves the problems or enables the client to better understand them and deal with them.

But there is another side to this. As I indicated above, healthy attributes as well as problems are related to past-life experience. Carol learned valuable lessons in her past lives, even the unhappy ones. In her very first life, the Ker life, although Ker was deformed by his illness and never quite accepted by his group, Carol said she had learned humor and just to enjoy living, and along her long way since then she has learned some things about leadership, and how to fit in with other people, and to stand up for what she believes, and to weigh the results of an action before she takes it, and various other very useful and necessary lessons. Along the way she learned to love, and to lose as well, and to endure and survive. In fact, "survival" was exactly what she said she had learned in El's sad life. And after her suicide as Antoinette, she said that she had not given the rest of her life the chance it deserved. This was one of the lessons she took away from that life: "to give life a chance, to wait and see what happens next."

These are all simple lessons, very practical, perhaps necessary for living life well but neither grandiose nor especially profound, certainly not "philosophical" or "spiritual" as we usually define those terms. It is as if living life well takes many skills, and one learns those skills over many centuries and lifetimes.

There is still another side. In all past lives, the past-life personality is a real personality, with emotions, relationships, responses, strengths, and weaknesses, and any and all of these seem to be available to the person today if he or she wants them. For example, sometime after she reported her past-life as Jean-Pierre, Carol discovered she had to give a talk in one of her classes, and the very thought of it frightened her. But during her past-life experience as Jean-Pierre, a strong, able man, and no shrinking violet when it came to speaking his mind in public, she had felt his strength and courage, his ability and willingness to speak up and be heard. She decided to give her talk as Jean-Pierre would have given it. When she gave the talk, she remembered the way Jean-Pierre's strength had felt during her regression and she drew that strength into herself.

She gave a talk that won her praise from the teacher and the other students alike, and she herself felt comfortable and actually enjoyed the experience. Most importantly, she had found the key to handling any other such talks in the future, and no longer feared them. She knew she could do it, and do it well. She had realized that Jean-Pierre's strength was really her own, and she could use it as she liked.

There are very specific connections between what we learn in our past lives and what we are today; one can say that what we are today is largely the cumulative growth we have experienced over our past lives. We are born with certain aptitudes, interests, approaches to life, fears, talents, tendencies to form good or bad relationships, desires to dominate or desires to be submissive, and all the other traits that make up human beings. Which of these we act upon and which we ignore seems to depend on our upbringing and the social conditions we are born and raised in.

One thing that we do not see in Carol's series or in past lives in general is retributive "karma." It is possible to define karma as precisely the sort of ongoing growth we do see, but this is a new and modern definition. We do not find the old reward-and-punishment model of karma in past-life regressions. I discuss this issue in more detail in Chapter 14.

Carol's series of past lives gives us a sense of the sequences of lives that people live. I have one other complete series, and although Carol's is of course unique to her, it is similar to the other in its overall patterns. Through our past lives there runs the thread of an increasing intricacy of personality, of more choices of ways to be, of living and learning, literally.

But there seems to be a strong element of luck involved, too: we choose what we hope will be a good family for us but we can't be sure; we hope for a healthy body, but again we take our chances; we hope for a decent life situation in which to grow and live and carry out our goals, but as usual, life has no guarantees. When we make the choice to return, we become the hostages of whatever events occur, such as a bad deal genetically, the early death of parents, poverty, a catastrophe of nature, an accident, an illness, a war. But a glance at Carol's past lives tells us that even in a bad situation we adapt, we usually learn something, although it may not be the lesson we think we came back in to learn. When we come back in, we accept what life gives us, and we make the best of it. And somehow, if we live long enough, we learn from it and take what we've learned on into our next life. And perhaps that is the most important lesson of all.

As for Carol, she says she enjoyed exploring her past lives, and learned many things from them, but that the greatest things she learned are that she is a "citizen of the planet," that life is to be lived with creativity, courage, and humor, and that she can trust herself to find her own best way to be.

CHAPTER FOURTEEN

PAST LIVES, RELIGIONS, AND PSYCHOLOGY

In Chapter 1, I presented a brief survey of the beliefs of various reincarnationist religious systems. It seems clear that past-life narratives do not support many of the beliefs of those systems. For example, many systems hold that only Great Souls, or only men, or only the nobility, or some other special group reincarnate at all. However, we have seen that this is not the picture from past-life regressions. We all seem to reincarnate, and over and over, and although in one life we may be a woman of high social status, in another we may be a simple male laborer.

Some systems hold that we reincarnate a certain number of times: three, or seven, or some other number. This may well be true, but if so, it is a number over, say, fifty, because a few of my own clients have said, when their Upper Mind was asked, that they had lived forty-five or so past lives. But this is rare. When the Upper Mind is asked, the number is more likely in the teens or twenties; the average seems to be somewhere in that range. Not all past-life therapists ask their clients this; most do not. I only ask when a client specifically wants to know, so what I say here is very shaky and should not be taken as the result of any organized research on my part. But there does not seem to be any particular, preordained number of lives that we all must live.

Occasionally you hear that some person claims to have lived thousands of lives, or to have lived "forever." Psychics often tell their clients these things and their clients believe them: They are "old souls." But as a past-life therapist, I do not see this. Instead, when asked for the number, clients' Upper Minds give a number between two and fifty.

Some systems hold that people reincarnate as animals, sometimes in a progression of lives leading up from animal to human state. There is also a new notion around that people sometimes say they have come to Earth from another planet, and that their first lives were on that other planet. But in past-life regressions, it is very rare for people to report past lives as animals, or extraterrestrial aliens either. There are a few cases of this in the literature, but I myself have never heard one.

It is perfectly possible to instruct a person in a trance state to imagine a "past life" as an animal or an alien, or even a plant, and this is sometimes deliberately done in the course of consciousness-raising therapies or shamanic workshops. These exercises are used as a means of fostering an awareness of the connectedness of all life forms, and they can be very meaningful. But without specific instructions to do so, people do not usually report these things in past-life regressions.

It is possible that we would not be able to recall a past life as an animal or a plant because in that life we would have had no language. But none of my clients has ever even hinted that there was some hidden animal or plant life in the wings. It is also possible that we reached humanhood only after many lives as animals, and this idea might actually fit within an evolutionary model of reincarnation. According to evolution, we did, after all, physically develop from a more primitive species, and our souls may have done the same. But when I ask clients to go back to their first lives, that life is invariably a human one on this planet, although sometimes in a primitive situation. The earliest life I have heard was in around 4000 B.C.E., although it was not a primitive life.

Some reincarnation systems hold that people reincarnate only into their own genetic families. This, like so many other beliefs about reincarnation, is not supported by past-life regressions. In fact, it seems to be fairly rare. People often do say they chose one of their parents because they had known this person in a prior life, but the relationship may not have been a genetic, family one. The two families involved, the past life family and the present one, may be on different continents and of two entirely different family lines.

In Chapters 7 and 12, I discussed the various relationships people say they have had in prior lives with people they know now in their present ones. While some of these relationships have been within the same genetic family, most have not. Carol said that she had chosen her present father because she had known him as a friend in her sixteenth-century life as Miguelo, but there was no genetic connection between the two families involved. Others say that they chose a parent because in a past life they had been a parent or other relative of the person who is now their parent, but these two families usually have no genetic connection.

Like the ideas above, the idea that people reincarnate only into their own families is not supported by past-life regressions. An exception seems to be that when continuing an old relationship is the goal, and the other person is still living, a person may choose to make a relatively fast return to life, perhaps as that person's child, grandchild, or sibling.

Karma is also a vital part of some religious reincarnation systems, and it is usually defined as a system of rewards and punishments for good and bad actions that works from one life to the next. The best way to assess this is to examine one person's complete series of past lives, as we examined Carol's fourteen past lives in Chapter 13.

There seems to be no pattern of reward and punishment flowing through Carol's past lives or anyone else's, or if there is, it is not easy to see. Of course, one could always say that whatever unfortunate thing happened in any given lifetime was a punishment for something "bad" the person had done in some previous life, or that good circumstances were a reward for "good" actions in a prior life. However, if this is correct, the patterns are indiscernible, and the direct connections between those actions and their results are not identifiable. This does not mean they are not there, but no client has told me yet of any such reward or punishment mechanism acting blindly upon us from life to life, nor do I see any signs of it in past-life regressions. People may punish themselves for some past misdeed, but this punishment is self-chosen, not inflicted upon them by some omniscient judge or by blind fate.

It is sometimes said that only reincarnation and karma can explain life's injustices. Why do some people seem just born lucky, with good health and into a prosperous, happy family that raises them well and helps them make happy, productive lives for themselves, while others struggle just to stay alive? Karma explains this, of course; the unfortunate person is suffering because of some bad action committed in a past life, and the lucky one is enjoying a well-deserved reward for good actions. Some nonreincarnationist religions believe something that attempts to explain this kind of injustice in a similar way. For them, prosperity is a sign of God's "grace," and the poor and suffering, although they deserve our compassion, do not merit quite as much good fortune from God. At any rate, they have not merited God's grace or they, too, would be healthy and prosperous.

These theories that the world's unfortunates are suffering some deserved punishment for past sins whereas the lucky ones are being rewarded for past good actions, or that the prosperous have somehow pleased God and received his special grace, are pernicious ideas. They can lead to indifference toward human suffering, as they have done in many countries and for many centuries.

Furthermore, these theories are irrelevant to the discussion of whether or not karma actually occurs. Unsupported theories are as easily made as contradicted by another unsupported theory. What we actually see happening in past-life regression is more relevant. When we examine a complete series of one person's past lives, such as Carol's, karma, as defined by the theories, does not appear, nor does any possibility of special grace from God.

It may be comforting to some people to believe that suffering is well deserved, that the unfortunates are paying for past-life sins, but aside from the fact that this fatalistic belief removes our responsibility to try to help others, it is not supported by what we see in past-life regressions. As in Carol's series, what we see is a process of self-directed growth from life to life, always vulnerable to accidents. We make mistakes, we learn from those mistakes, and eventually we learn to make good lives for ourselves.

And the "good life" doesn't seem to have much to do with material wealth, status, or power. Instead, client after client says they learned the skills for living life in their various past lives. They learned how to love, to live in a family, to live alone, to create good relationships, to stand up for their beliefs, to laugh and enjoy life, to care for the suffering, to teach, to create, and sometimes just to survive terrible conditions. They learn all manner of useful skills like that, as I have described in the chapters of this book. But they do not say these past lives or the lessons they learn from them are imposed upon them; they themselves learn them from the conditions of their past lives. And those conditions seem to have no karmic basis.

As I said in Chapter 11, we take our chances when we come into a life, and we learn whatever we find to learn. Aside from the idea of reincarnation itself, very few of the details of religious reincarnation systems are supported by what we see in past-life regressions.

One can ask just how those theories came into being in the first place. Since reincarnation is such an ancient belief and its origins are buried far back in the mists of time, we cannot be certain how or where the belief itself began. But one can speculate that belief in reincarnation began very early in human history because people had hunches, dreams, and déjà vu experiences just as we do, or because tiny children spoke of their prior lives just as they do today. There may have been some recalls of past lives in states of trance, too; trances are commonly achieved in the dancing and other rituals of traditional peoples even today.

But whatever the source of the belief itself, the only theories about reincarnation that we know about have all been recorded by extremely sophisticated, literate people who wrote those theories down. Most of those writings are beautiful literature, true works of art and genius, often sheer poetry. But they are only theories, nevertheless. In some cases, the writers may have developed their theories from mystical, self-induced trance states; in others the theories may faithfully reflect what the prevailing culture already believed, or even what some religious system or government found most useful at the time. But the writers, often anonymous, were educated, sophisticated people centuries removed from the primitive origins of the belief in reincarnation itself.

One thing that seems clear is that the religious theories were not developed by examining hypnotically facilitated past-life regressions and constructing the theories accordingly. If that had been done, the theories would be very different than they are. As it is, we can accept the old theories only in the fundamental belief in reincarnation, but as for most of the details of those theories, we will have to jettison them except as enduring literature and lovely mythology.

What, then, about the theories of psychology? In Chapter 2, I gave a brief overview of the main trends of psychology as it has developed in our century, from Freud to postmodern psychology. To some extent, as I have said in earlier chapters, what we see in past-life regressions looks like behaviorism in action. In Carol's series of past lives, she learns "lessons," or attitudes and beliefs, from each life through its particular experiences, and she carries those "lessons" into the next life.

We see behaviorism even more clearly in the other past-life stories in this book. All the phobias, depressions, compulsions, relationship patterns, aches and pains, all the problems that people come for therapy for, seem to have developed from repeated negative past experiences, and sometimes those experiences occurred in the present life and sometimes in one or more past lives. Either way, the negative experiences accumulated over time, whether that time was the few decades since the person's birth or centuries since the relevant past lives. This is essentially the process of reinforcement, whether negative or positive, the fundamental tenet of behaviorism: we learn what is reinforced by our experiences, and the more experiences that reinforce a given belief or action, the stronger the learning, whether positive or negative.

Although behaviorism can help to explain the process of learning and the development of problems and positive attributes that occur over past lives, the richness and complexity of the past lives themselves that people report are not easily explained by behaviorism or any other form of modern psychology. The usual "conventional" explanation for past-life narratives is that these stories are generated by the imagination drawing upon the many books, movies, and other stories that we have all been exposed to in our complex society. Although we may not always realize it, today we all have an immense amount of random historical knowledge, learned not only from our formal educations but also from all those books, movies, and television stories we have read and seen. How easy it would be, it may seem, to construct a fantasy based upon that information.

The only thing wrong with this explanation is that the actual past lives that people report are usually not placed in the historical times or places that are most familiar to us or that are the settings for any books or movies that can be found. Often they are set in times and places that can be found only in some obscure, dusty reference book on a forgotten library shelf, if at all. Nor do the past-life stories themselves reflect the characters or plots of any books or movies.

To use one of Carol's past lives as an example, her fourth life, as Marcus, although set in ancient Rome, was set in the sixth century, a time period that has been largely ignored by history books, historical novels, and moviemakers. In most people's minds, by the sixth century Rome had been "fallen" for two centuries, and the Goths were villains who had wrecked the city. Carol herself, before she recalled the Marcus life, believed these things. Yet Marcus tells us another story, and when I checked the dusty history books, I found his story was a true reflection of what really happened.

The Goths, who much admired Roman civilization, had allowed religious freedom and had done much to rebuild Rome's fortunes, and its ancient temples as well, during their rulership. But when the Goths lost control to the Eastern Empire, the people of Rome lost their religious freedom, and a period of chaos ensued. A severe Christianity was reinstated, the "pagan" temples were destroyed, and dissidents were persecuted and punished exactly as Marcus and his family were, by confiscation of their estates and other property, impoverishment, and execution. Even the issue Marcus and his family came to grief over, refusing to acknowledge the divinity of the Emperor, was a major issue of the time and did, indeed, cost the lives and fortunes of many Roman families like Marcus's.

In a way, if past-life stories are imagination at work, one might ask why Carol did not report a past life in the earlier and much better known ancient Rome of movies and books, perhaps one in which she was a Christian thrown to Nero's lions, or a senator gathering with his peers in the Forum, possibly even one who participated in the murder of Caesar: Why not? Or why not one of the emperors, for that matter? Our imaginations are fully capable of creating such romances, so why don't we do this in our past-life stories? None of Carol's characters can be found in books or movies, nor can their life stories. Yet she knows as much about history as any of us, and should have been able to draw upon that knowledge to create more adventurous scenarios. In a way, the very humdrum quality of past-life stories, the simple humanness of the characters, and the obscure times and places that are usually, as in Carol's series, the settings, all make a case for the reality of past-life stories as memories, not imagined romances.

In any case, considering past-life stories the products of imagination does not explain them, because imagination itself has not been well explained by psychology. Certainly human beings have always been storytellers and mythmakers. Our literature is rich with our narrative inventions. But no one has really figured out what causes this creativity. It is one of the great mysteries of humankind.

Furthermore, we all have the capacity to role-play, to some extent at least. One of the beliefs of postmodern psychology is that we all play roles, the roles that our culture expects of us. In fact, as far as any individual life goes, whether past or present, this seems true: People do learn to behave in whatever ways the culture of the time and place expects them to. Other postmodern psychologists have suggested that reporting past-life stories is in itself an exercise in creative role-playing. But one should consider the larger fact that few people brought up in our Western world were raised to believe in reincarnation and to play the roles of obscure people who have been long dead, and then claim that they "were" those people in their prior lives. Our Western culture does not expect this of them, and yet they report those past lives.

But in the processes of past-life development, we do see something like what humanistic psychology teaches. According to humanistic psychology, essentially we grow ourselves. We have an inborn impulse to grow and develop and change toward health, although that impulse can be thwarted or distorted by our environment, especially our upbringing. We see this process in Carol's past-life series, as she learns, grows, and changes over the centuries, becoming increasingly more complex and wiser—and more questioning—as she moves from life to life. We see it in all past-life narratives, as people say they learned valuable lessons from each life in its turn and take those lessons with them into the next life.

Behaviorism can explain the mechanisms of how we learn whatever we learn—that life is good, that bees are nice, that heights are frightening, that we can build good relationships, and all the other lessons, positive or negative, that we bring along from life to life. But the processes of growth and change over lifetimes seem to reflect the theories of personal growth of humanistic and transpersonal psychologies. And the fact that people recall past lives that are so often different from their present selves, different in gender, nationality, religion, skin color, social status, and all the other human attributes, reflects transpersonal and postmodern views of human beings as having the capacity to go beyond their narrow individual identities and to identify with others.

All of these conventional psychological schools, of course, like other mainstream theories, consider past-life narratives imagination, and their theories are based upon and apply to our present life only, assumed to be our only life. But some of the same theories can easily be extended to include the learning and growth processes of our past as well as our present lives, although many mainstream psychologists might argue with doing so.

There is another set of theories that seem relevant, although they do not explain past-life stories. Freud and Jung, and other early psychoanalysts, held that we have an unconscious part of our mind that shapes our life, and in this general proposition they seem to be correct, although perhaps not in the details. Perhaps part of that "unconscious" remembers our past lives, and brings them into consciousness through dreams, flashbacks, déjà vu experiences, and induced trance states like hypnosis. It may also create our problems and our joys as our unconscious memories of what we have learned in our past lives push us to action and shape the way we construct our selves. In other words, perhaps our "unconscious" itself is composed in part of all our "forgotten" past-life memories.

However, the specific theories of the early psychoanalysts are not recognizably reflected in past-life stories. For example, the idea that past-life stories are creations of the imagination cannot be explained by Freud's theories about creativity. Freud considered imagination and creative productions as reflecting suppressed desires or, in the case of art, the ability of the artist to sort of "dip down" into the primitive id and capture the raw emotions stored there, "bringing them back" as art. This explanation of imagination and creative productions is intriguing, but it does not begin to explain what we see in past-life stories. If it did, we would see much more raw violence and uncontrolled behavior than we see in past-life stories, and many fewer "real" people. The idea that we are merely expressing our suppressed desires seems incorrect, too, because our past-life stories are so mundane, and usually much less glorious than we had hoped or imagined they might be before we went into hypnosis and found them.

Nor do Jung's theories about the unconscious seem particularly relevant. As I discussed in Chapter 2, Jung held that we all carry in our unconscious what he called the "collective unconscious," a collection of mythic figures that are based upon the historical and mythic experiences of the whole human race. Jung's collective unconscious consists of certain fundamental types, the archetypes: the wise child, the shadow, the *persona*, the *anima/animus*, the Self, and others. I defined some of these in Chapter 2; others are self-explanatory. According to Jung, these unconscious archetypes act out their dramas in various ways.

All of this may well be true, but it does not support any claims that past-life stories are imagination at work, because no past-life story that I know of reflects any particular archetype. However, if Jung is correct, and if our past-life characters were real people, then they would have carried the collective unconscious in their personal unconscious just as we ourselves would. But people do not produce any specific, identifiable archetypes as their past-life personalities. What they produce are recognizable human beings, living their lives as best they can. If in the process they go through childhood into maturity and age, and are of one gender or the other, so do we all, and Jung's archetypes are as applicable to them as to ourselves, neither more so nor less.

Some past-life therapists who are also Jungians have suggested that the "collective unconscious" exists as a sort of inborn awareness of all the lives that have ever been lived, rather than being a collection of archetypes as Jung suggested. According to these theorists, people dip into this "pool of all past lives" when they produce a past-life story, choosing a life that is of special interest and relevance to their personal concerns. In other words, the past lives they report have been lived, but by other, long-gone people; they themselves have not really lived those lives.

Some consider this pool to be inborn, perhaps genetic; others tie the idea to concepts of parallel universes or similar theoretical models of reality. However, there is little evidence for any of these ideas. Although they are intriguing, they seem unnecessarily complicated. If such a collective pool could exist at all, it would have to be based upon some abstract form of memory that not only remembered the events of people's lives after they were dead, but also then pooled them together with all other people's lives. People accessing past lives would then have to scan the immense pool of all those billions of past lives for one that met their needs and report it as their own. This seems considerably more complicated and harder to explain than the simpler and more straightforward explanation that the past lives people report are personal to themselves, as people themselves say they are.

There are more telling arguments against this idea of a collective pool of all the lives that have ever been lived. They are mostly arguments from logic; obviously, no research has been done about this and it is hard to know just how any *could* be done. But to me, one problem is that people report such ordinary lives. One would think that, given the choice among all the billions of lives that have ever been lived, all "stored" somewhere in a memory pool of lives, people would choose more interesting lives; perhaps lives of famous or important people, or lives in the midst of some important historical event. As I have said, this is extremely rare. Even if people confine their choice to a life that is relevant to whatever problems or issues they want to explore, there would still be an enormous group of historically interesting lives from which to select, because there are, after all, a limited number of possible human problems and issues, and a good many people down the ages have suffered from all of them.

For example, a depressed man or a compulsive woman could doubtless find some long-dead king or queen who had some experience that could explain the clients' problems. This should be much more interesting and satisfying to the client than the life of an obscure peasant. Yet it is the obscure peasant's life that the client is much more apt to report.

The other problem with the idea of the "pool" of all lives ever lived is that people who explore all of their past lives do not usually give dates that overlap. When there are two overlapping dates, the person has usually guessed at one or both dates. They have either been asked the dates during the regression itself, or cannot clearly see one of the dates on the imaginary screen. Either way, the person will guess if simply asked what they think it is, and they know they are guessing and say so. And even then the dates do not usually overlap.

Logic says that if people had access to some collective pool of lives from which to select any past lives that met their needs, they would often select lives that overlap in dates, especially when they do not explore the lives chronologically. In such cases, there is really no sensible reason that they should pay any attention to the dates of the lives they "borrow" from the pool. Yet overlapping dates are rare if the date is found without the person being put in a position in which they feel they have to guess. This is, of course, one of the reasons I ask clients' Upper Minds to place dates and other factual information on an imaginary screen after the lifetime has been explored. The information simply appears, and clients read it off and do not have to guess.

For all these reasons, I believe that the idea of a "pool" of all the lives that have ever been lived is most likely incorrect. First, it is simply not supported by what we see in past-life regressions or in any other way, and second, it requires a much more intricate model of reality than is necessary to explain what we actually *do* see in past-life regressions. What is known as "Occam's Razor" is very relevant here. Occam's Razor is one of the guiding principles of science— and of daily life, too, for that matter—and it says that explanations should not be more complicated than they need to be. The idea of a pool of all lives is a much more complicated idea than we need to explain what happens in past-life regressions.

Modern psychology has given us some theories that do help, especially those of behaviorism, humanistic psychology, transpersonal psychology, and postmodern psychology. What we actually see happening in past-life regressions supports some of their theories, if the theories are extended to include past-life experiences. As we continue to explore past-life regressions, we may find that other theories of modern psychology are supported as well.

Past-Life Therapy

Past-life therapy shares some theories and methods with all of the psychological systems above, and differs in some ways as well. Perhaps the most important thing to notice is that past-life therapy supports Freud's most basic idea that many of our thoughts, feelings, and actions—our personalities, if you like—are indeed affected strongly by something like an unconscious mind of which we are normally entirely unaware. Past-life regressions have shown us that when we delve into that level of the mind in hypnosis, we find a personal history that may reach back centuries; and we find that what we learned in those other lives we have never really forgotten, not in that unconscious part of our minds. Instead we have carried all those experiences as lessons and have learned from them. Some of the lessons we have carried result in problems today, and some result in helpful, productive attributes. But they all seem stored in our unconscious minds.

We also find that the ideas of Jung, Adler, and Maslow about individuation, the life journey, and self-actualization seem to be correct for us. We try, all along the way, to make the best of our unconscious inheritance from our past lives. Past-life therapy tries to help people do that.

We also see that transpersonal psychology allows us to take our subjective spiritual experiences, such as past-life memories, seriously. No one really knows whether past-life stories are real memories or fantasies, but they are real for the person reporting them, and from the standpoint of transpersonal psychology, that's enough. According to the theories of transpersonal psychology, past-life regressions are spiritual experiences, and thus by definition they are healing. The question of whether they are real reincarnation memories or fantasies is of secondary importance to their therapeutic value.

Perhaps surprisingly, we also find that the behaviorists and the cognitive theorists are on the right track, too. However, like the other theorists, they have considered only one life, the present one, in their research and in developing their theories. Past-life therapy suggests that they have worked with too narrow a view; we learn through reinforcements in all our lives, and we carry what we learn on into all our subsequent lives, for good or ill. Cognitive theory holds that as we think, so we are; so that a man who has learned, or been conditioned, as behaviorists would say, to fear bees through negative experiences has made a decision, had a thought, that bees are frightening. Past-life therapy shows us that this decision may be made in a past life, following a bad experience with bees, after which the man will believe in his next life that bees are dangerous and will react to them with fear and a panic attack.

In the same way, it may be that the reason the phobia disappears after the man examines his past lives is that he now knows the reason for the phobia, recognizes that he has no particular need to fear bees in this life, and can cease to fear them. All this reverses the earlier decision he made, thus changing his thoughts about bees, and thinking differently about bees removes his fear of them. In cognitive therapy this is called "reframing," although most cognitive therapists work with only the present life. But this basic process of reframing may well be what happens in past-life therapy.

Throughout this book, I have briefly discussed elements of various theories of psychology as they are reflected in the past lives I discuss. There are many similarities, and many differences, as well. Past-life therapy and the psychological theories that arise from it knit the work of a century of psychology together to create a new form of psychology, reincarnation psychology. Reincarnation psychology can be considered the cluster of theories that arises from what we see in past-life regressions and therapy. Basically, what we see happening in past-life regressions and therapy supports some of the theories of all schools of psychology, and does not support other theories. For those it does support, reincarnation psychology extends the theories to include events and experiences from our past lives as well as from our present lives.

A good many mainstream psychologists, however, would balk at this, claiming that we "know" that there is no soul or any other part of a human being that can survive death, let alone move along to inhabit another body and live another life. For them, the whole idea of reincarnation is nothing more than a mystical concept and a religious delusion.

One must always examine basic assumptions, and in this case the basic assumption is stated pretty clearly above: "We know that there is no soul or any other part of a human being that can survive death, let alone move along to inhabit another body and live another life." The fact is, we do not know this at all. It is just an assumption. Science has never proved it, although many people seem to think it has. In fairness, in the past it has been hard to know how science would either prove it or disprove it. But today, past life regressions offer us a way to examine the truth of this statement, for if we find through research that the past-life stories that people report are true memories of other lives, then it follows logically that there must be some part of the human being that can, indeed, survive death and go on to another life.

One danger with an assumption like the one above is that if you really believe it, you will not look for any evidence to the contrary. Why should you? You know this is true, therefore it is a waste of time (and the self-destruction of a perfectly good career) even to suggest that the assumption might be wrong. Yet today a good many "hard" scientists are beginning to entertain the idea that the assumption is, indeed, wrong, and entirely wrong, not just a little bit askew.

Thomas Kuhn, in his book *The Structure of Scientific Revolutions*, uses the concept of a "paradigm shift" to explain what happens when a major assumption of science topples. There have been many such paradigm shifts in history: the theories of Copernicus that the earth revolves around the sun and not vice versa; the discovery by Galileo of the moons of Jupiter and the circular motion of those moons around their planet; the relativity theories of Einstein, to name only three. All these ideas seem natural and obvious to us today; in fact, they have now become our own assumptions. But they all violated the basic assumptions of the science of their times, and all met major resistance. Yet after these ideas were finally accepted, they changed everybody's way of looking at the world. According to Kuhn, that's what a paradigm shift does.

Obviously, if past-life stories are real reincarnation memories, the effect upon our society would be massive. It would truly be a paradigm shift, by Kuhn's definition. There is a great deal of evidence that they are real; and it is easier to explain them if they are real than if they are not, because imagination does not really work for this. By now, too many past-life stories have been reported; too much research supports their reality; too many people have found the sources of their problems in past lives and thereby rid themselves of the problems; too many babbling toddlers have told their disbelieving elders about their past lives. So that old assumption may have to go, and we are faced with a new form of psychology, reincarnation psychology, as well as new challenges for creating a good world based upon the way reincarnation works.

Whether that good world will be a better world is up to us all. We face a great many problems right now, at the dawn of a new century and a new millennium. And unfortunately, past-life regressions show us a bloody, tumultuous history: war, cruelty, poverty, and destruction weave like bloodstained threads through the tapestry of our common past, and they are still weaving themselves into the pattern. The Four Horsemen of the Apocalypse, those old familiar figures from the Book of Revelation, have never ceased their efforts and they are as active today as ever. War, famine, pestilence, and plague are with us still and they will destroy us if we do not take immediate steps to stop them. What past-life regression shows us is that we ourselves are the horsemen, the riders, no one else. And only we can turn ourselves away from our destructive paths. As Pogo so wisely said, "We have met the enemy, and he is us."

Today we face all of the old problems above plus some new ones: our massive population increase and the resulting ecological disasters that threaten to destroy all life on our planet. But from the evidence of past-life regressions, this planet is our only home and only we can save it.

Paradoxically, and also from the evidence of past-life regressions, we all want and hope for a peaceful, productive world, one in which we live with others with love and caring, and in which we ourselves can grow and build for the future generations to come. Those generations are, of course, our children and ourselves, in a very real sense.

So I paraphrase Pogo and say, "We have met the future, and it is us." What kind of world we will return to is, indeed, up to us now. For what we build now, we will inhabit in the future. Or not.

BIBLIOGRAPHY

Bernstein, M. (1978). *The Search for Bridey Murphy.* New York: Pocket Books. (Original work published in 1956.)

Bowman, C. (1997). *Children's Past Lives: How Past-Life Memories Affect Your Child.* New York: Bantam Books.

Clark, R. L. (1995). *Past Life Therapy: The State of the Art.* Austin, TX: Rising Star Press.

Cranston, S., and Williams, C. (1993). *Reincarnation: A New Horizon in Science, Religion, and Society.* Pasadena, CA: Theosophical University Press.

de Jong, M. (1992). Agoraphobia: Trauma of a Lost Soul? *Journal of Regression Therapy,* VI(1).

Dubuc, P. (1996). Learning Through Happy Past Lives. *Journal of Regression Therapy,* X(1).

Freedman, T. B. (1991). Treating Children's Nightmares with Past Life Report Therapy: A Case and a Discussion. *Journal of Regression Therapy,* V(1).

Freedman, T. B. (1997). Past Life and Interlife Therapy of Phobic People: Patterns and Outcome. *Journal of Regression Therapy,* XI(1).

Fuqua, E. (1989). Using Past-Life Concepts in Child Therapy. *Journal of Regression Therapy,* IV(1).

Head, J., and Cranston. S.L. (1977). *Reincarnation: The Phoenix Fire Mystery.* New York: Julian/Crown.

Hoffmann, A. (1993). Past Life Induced Anorexia: A Case Study. *Journal of Regression Therapy,* VII(1).

James, R. (1993). Regressed Past Lives and Survival After Physical Death: A Unique Experience? *Journal of Regression Therapy,* VII(1).

Kelsey, D., and Grant, J. (1969). *Many Lifetimes.* New York: Pocket Books.

Krippner, S. (1987). Folk Healing Traditions and Past-Life Therapies. *Journal of Regression Therapies,* II(2).

Krippner, S. (1994). Past-Life Report Therapy in the Treatment of Multiple Personality Disorders by Kardicist Healers in Brazil. *Journal of Regression Therapy,* VIII(1).

Shapiro, A. (1992). "ProLove" and the Ensoulement Dilemma. *Journal of Regression Therapy,* VI(1).

Stevenson, I. (1987). *Children Who Remember Previous Lives: A Question of Reincarnation.* Charlottesville, VA: University Press of Virginia.

Stevenson, I. (1997). *Reincarnation and Biology: A Contribution to the Etiology of Birthmarks and Birth Defects.* Two volumes, hardcover. Westport, CT: Praeger.

Stevenson, I. (1997). *Where Reincarnation and Biology Intersect.* Synopsis of above, one volume, paperback. Westport, CT: Praeger.

van der Maesen, R. (1998). PLT for Giles De La Tourette's Syndrome: A Research Study. *Journal of Regression Therapy,* XII(1).

van der Maesen, R. (1999). PLT and Hallucinated Voices: A Research Study. *Journal of Regression Therapy,* XIII(1).

van der Maesen, R. (1998). PLT for Giles De La Tourette's Syndrome: A Research Study. *Journal of Regression Therapy,* XII(1).

Wambach, H. (1978). *Reliving Past Lives: The Evidence Under Hypnosis.* New York: Harper & Row.

INDEX

THELMA BEACH FREEDMAN, PH.D.

Thelma Beach Freedman, Ph.D., has a B.S. degree in education and an M.A. and Ph.D. in clinical psychology. She has studied clinical hypnotherapy at the Hypnosis Consulting Center, the Association for the Advancement of Ethical Hypnosis, and the Association for Past Life Research and Therapies. She has practiced hypnotherapy and past-life therapy for over twenty years. The former director of Hypnosis Associates, in Dewitt, New York, she offers a training course in past-life therapy for professionals. Her M.A. thesis and Ph.D. dissertation were in the fields of hypnotherapy and past life therapy, and she has conducted research and published articles in those areas. She served four years on the Board of Directors of the Association for Past Life Research and Therapies, now called the International Association for Regression Research and Therapies (IARRT). She is a former research chairperson for that organization and a former editor of the *Journal of Regression Therapy*. At the present time she is the president of the International Board for Regression Therapy, the accrediting organization for past life therapists and training programs. She also conducts a private practice in hypnotherapy and past-life therapy and presents group workshops in past-life regression.